W9-APH-553

tools for rebuilding

To
Father John
with blessings !

Michael

"Wow! This is a powerful and immensely readable field guide for everyone who wants to transform their church. Whether you're the pastor in charge, a part-time volunteer, or one of the numerous individuals who labor in the middle, *Tools for Rebuilding* is a must-have resource. Implementing even a few of the ideas here could make a huge difference in bringing more people to Christ."

Patrick Lencioni
Author of *The Five Dysfunctions of a Team*

"This book is a must-read for anyone who is involved in the great work of parish ministry. It's chock-full of practical wisdom and enlightening answers to the questions we all face concerning the spiritual health of our parishes and the effectiveness of our outreach."

Cardinal Seán O'Malley
Archbishop of Boston

"In a friendly and accessible style, the authors of *Tools for Rebuilding* help pastors and parish staff members take a fresh look at many dimensions of parish life and shape them in ways that will bring people closer to the Lord—the ultimate goal of all parish life."

Cardinal Francis George
Archbishop of Chicago

"As thought-provoking as the authors' first book, *Rebuilt*, this sequel provides ways to revitalize the American parish. Not everyone will agree with or implement everything, but everyone who reads this important book will come away with a lot to think about, pray over, and use in day-to-day pastoral ministry. A must-read and a must-discuss for parish ministers!"

Msgr. Kevin Irwin
Former Dean of the School of Theology and Religious Studies
Catholic University of America

"An insightful and compelling collection of practical ideas and strategies sure to bring fresh life to parish engagement and renewal. Read and let the weaving of scripture, story, and down-to-earth initiatives enrich, expand, and deepen your parish leadership efforts."

Sister Edith Prendergast, R.S.C.
Director of the Office of Religious Education
Archdiocese of Los Angeles

"Alleluia, they've done it again! Fr. Michael White and Mr. Tom Corcoran are two voices crying in the wilderness, 'It's not business as usual!' In *Rebuilt* they gave us hope that renewal was possible for a parish and a vision of what it could look like. In *Tools for Rebuilding*, they help Catholic parish leaders with wonderful tools to develop a strategy for renewal. Both things are vital, for vision without strategy is hallucination. There is no hallucination in this book but rather simple, pure, double-distilled wisdom that is aged more than fifteen years and is ready to pour and enjoy. It will inspire you, challenge you to your toes, and move you to get to work on the great task of the New Evangelization."

Rev. James Mallon
Pastor and Founder/Director of the John Paul II Media Institute

"I am very excited for this book! It won't make rebuilding your parish easy, but it will give you practical, tested, and doable steps to help you succeed when you're ready to work at doing Christ's mission."

Diana Macalintal
Director of Worship
Diocese of San Jose

"'Rebuild my church' was the charge given to Francis in the thirteenth century, but there was no road map. In our time, *Tools for Rebuilding* gives precisely that: practical guidelines for evangelization and forming disciples. An invaluable resource for parish leaders."

Zeni Fox
Professor of Pastoral Theology
Seton Hall University

tools for rebuilding

75 Really, Really
Practical Ways to Make
Your Parish Better

Michael White and Tom Corcoran

AVE MARIA PRESS AVE Notre Dame, Indiana

Scripture texts in this work are taken from the *New American Bible, revised edition* ©2011 Confraternity of Christian Doctrine, Washington, DC.

———————————————————————

© 2013 by Michael White and Tom Corcoran

All rights reserved. No part of this book may be used or reproduced in any manner whatsoever, except in the case of reprints in the context of reviews, without written permission from Ave Maria Press®, Inc., P.O. Box 428, Notre Dame, IN 46556, 1-800-282-1865.

Founded in 1865, Ave Maria Press is a ministry of the United States Province of Holy Cross.

www.avemariapress.com

Paperback: ISBN-10 1-59471-444-4, ISBN-13 978-1-59471-444-3

E-book: ISBN-10 1-59471-445-2, ISBN-13 978-1-59471-445-0

Cover and text design by John Carson.

Printed and bound in the United States of America.

Library of Congress Cataloging-in-Publication Data is available.

CONTENTS

Preface xi

Introduction: Building 1

Strategic Tools

1. Don't Just Do Something, Stand There 11
2. And Then, Focus 17
3. Know Why, What, and How 20
4. Clearly Define Evangelization 25
5. Pull Down the Silos 28
6. You (Probably) Need More Gratitude and Enthusiasm 31
7. The NFL Is the Enemy of the Church 34

Building Tools

8. Sometimes It's Okay Not to Be Generous 41
9. Did Anyone Unlock the Front Door? 45
10. I'm Not Interested in How Much You Love Jesus;
    Just Clean Your Nursery 48
11. Christmas Is Over, So Throw Out the Dead Poinsettias ... 52
12. Be a Control Freak (But Only about Your Building) 55

Office Tools

13. Foot Traffic and Phone Calls Do Not Prove
    You're Relevant 63
14. Break Up the "Nests" 66
15. Empty Your Own Trash Can 68

Communication Tools

16. Stop Advertising (Other People's Stuff) in Your Bulletin 73
17. You Are Your Website 76
18. "Look, They Have a 'Kidzone' Too!" 79
19. Connect with Your Community 83

People Tools

20. Know Who's Not Here 89
21. Vestments Are Like Golf Clubs 92
22. Churchpeople Don't Belong in the Pews 94

Weekend Tools

23. Greet Guests 99
24. Remember All That Money You Saved on Vestments? 101
25. Invest in Music 103
26. Nobody Is Growing in Christ Just Because of
    Your Pious Procession of One 106
27. Manage the Transitions 110
28. Take People on a Journey 113
29. Know What Season You're In 116

Preaching Tools

30. Find Your Message; Then Stay on It 123
31. One Church, One Message 126
32. Comfort Outsiders/Challenge Insiders 130
33. Preach the Announcements 134

Sacramental Tools

34. Baptisms Are Opportunities—Take Them 139
35. When It Comes to First Communion,
    Put Down the Carrot and Stick 143
36. Make Confirmation Initiation, Not Graduation 147
37. People Really Will Come to Confession—Really 152
38. Use Anointing Strategically 155
39. Beware of Self-Righteous Super Consumers 158
40. Seriously, See What Happens When
    You Stop Announcing Mass Intentions 162
41. Funerals Are Scud Missiles 167

Kids and Students Tools

42. Do Something for My Kids, You Do Something for Me .. 175
43. After Second Grade, School Isn't Cool 179
44. Treat Students Like Adults 183

Money Tools

45. Fundraisers Create Sideways Energy 189
46. Pass the Basket as Seldom as Possible 193
47. Seal Up the Poor Boxes 196
48. Losers Go for Fruit 199
49. Know How to Ask for Money 202
50. Shape the Path 205
51. Be Responsible/Be Transparent 208

Staff Tools

52. Widen the Gene Pool 213
53. Get the Right People on the Bus 216
54. Talent Attracts Talent 220
55. Work Weekends 222
56. Be Leaders Who Learn 224

Critical Tools

57. Prepare for Battle 231
58. Cards Are Good; Letters Are Bad 234
59. Don't Be Upset When the Wrong People Leave 237
60. Don't Be Surprised When the Right People Leave 240
61. Say You're Wrong When You're Wrong;
    Say You're Sorry (Even When You're Not) 243
62. Admit You Don't Know What You're Doing 246
63. Get Over It 249

Fun Tools

64. Celebrate Wins 255
65. Because a Win Belongs to Everyone 258
66. What Gets Rewarded Gets Repeated 260
67. Have Fun 263

Overall Tools

68. Father, It's Not All About You 269
69. Be an Authority 273
70. Everything Takes Longer Than You Think 276
71. There Are No Silver Bullets 279
72. Seek Wise Counsel 282

73. Christmas Eve Is Paradigm for Everything 286
74. It's Not an Air War; It's a Trench War 291
75. Stop Trying to Make People Go to Church,
    and Make Church Matter 294

PREFACE

In the first book, Theophilus . . .
—Acts of the Apostles 1:1

Even the best-known and most famous authors sometimes feel the
need to explain why they are writing more. Readers of our first book,
Rebuilt, might be asking that question. St. Luke's short answer in
the Acts of the Apostles, his sequel to the Gospel of Luke, was, well,
because there's more to tell.

When we wrote *Rebuilt* and published it in early 2013, we sought
to cover a wide spectrum of parish life and ministry with broad strokes.
While every attempt was made to leave the reader with practical help
and hope, the emphasis was definitely on the big picture, the story we
had to tell, and we're glad we did it that way.

But there's more to tell. The story told in *Rebuilt* is not the end of
our story. As we stepped back from the project, and especially as we
began talking with our readers, we recognized that there was interest,
even hunger, for more practical information on what works, what
helps, what specific steps we took, and which tools we used to grow
disciples, develop a healthier parish community, and more intentionally and effectively serve the New Evangelization.

As we try with this book to further engage readers of *Rebuilt*, we also eagerly welcome readers unfamiliar with that book who are simply interested in "really, really practical ways to make your parish better." Here you will find exactly seventy-five such ways, touching on virtually every aspect of parish life. And they're mostly free.

We offer *Tools for Rebuilding* for those who are interested in their local church community, which Catholics call their parish. Here we present simple lessons that were for a variety of reasons not so simple for us to learn. Each of them represents a step forward for our parish and an important recognition of a better way of *doing* church by focusing on *building* church. Whether you are a pastor or pastoral leader, parish minister, consecrated religious, deacon, seminarian, or interested parishioner, these lessons can be useful to you in your community. We suspect that many of them will be useful to leaders in other settings as well.

We are presenting our practical approaches in the form of axioms. These are reasonable claims that are evidently true—at least to those who have learned their lessons through hard-earned experience. These are reasonable claims, and yet, where not honored, they easily become stumbling blocks and sources of conflict and division in parishes. Little things become big things and get in the way of our work. You won't agree with everything we assert, and that's okay. We just want to further the conversation. Take a look.

Introduction:

BUILDING

They devoted themselves to the teaching of
the apostles and to the communal life, to the
breaking of the bread and to the prayers. Awe
came upon everyone, and many wonders
and signs were done through the apostles.
—Acts 2:42–43

The Church of Christ, in its earliest, purest, and most exuberant
period—the age of the apostles—is described in the first chapters of
the fifth book of the New Testament. St. Luke, who wrote the Acts of
the Apostles, tells us how the Holy Spirit begins shaping the Church
through the apostolic ministry. More than any other way, we learn that
these efforts are fruitful in two ways: introducing people to Christ and
helping them grow into fully devoted followers, that is, disciples, of
the Lord. In exactly these ways they advanced the movement of the
kingdom of God in their generation.

This is always and everywhere the fundamental and indispensible
work of the whole Church. Currently fueled by the imperative of the
New Evangelization, it is about bringing the Gospel to those who

have not heard it, or need to hear it again. And then, it is about helping them grow into fully devoted disciples of Jesus Christ, especially
through the Word of God and the Eucharist.

Probably nobody disputes that. The difficulty comes when we reach
down into the details of building or rebuilding the Church of Christ.
The legendary architect Mies van der Rohe is sometimes credited with
claiming that in any building project, "the devil's in the detail." The
detail is where all of us in "churchworld" can begin to look at things
very differently. It's also where we can get mixed up about what we're
even trying to do.

And, because of what it is we're supposed to be building, that's a
problem.

Your Building Site

If you're going to build anything, anywhere, you need to start somewhere, specific; you need a building site.

"Parish" is a geographical term; it is a location. It comes from the
Greek *paroikia*, which refers to a collection of neighboring buildings.
Your parish is a neighborhood, however compact or far flung it is.
And your neighborhood is where you join the Lord in building the
movement of the kingdom.

To be successful in building, you have to know your parish, because
that's your building site. Your parish—not just your congregation but
your parish—actually includes people you don't even know, people
who currently aren't in the pews.

We don't know anything about your parish, but let us tell you about
ours. Church of the Nativity is essentially equivalent to the 21093 zip
code, a choice slice of north Baltimore County. Maryland is called
"the land of pleasant living," and it must be because of places like our
parish. There are lots of things we could tell you about this community
that might interest you, but here's a fact that might surprise you: The

majority of people in our parish do not go to church—and they're Catholic. They don't go to church because they don't like the experience, they don't understand the Eucharist, and they're not interested in learning why they should. And no amount of wishing it was otherwise or demanding that it be different will change that fact.

In order to successfully begin building, then, we had to humbly learn about why they have left and what might bring them back.

Your Building Project

But what are we building? Churches . . . right? Well, kind of right.

At one point in his public ministry, Jesus takes his twelve disciples on a road trip. It's one of the biggest journeys of his adult life and probably farther than any of the disciples would have ventured on their own. They go to an unlikely destination: Caesarea Philippi, which was sort of an ancient Las Vegas on steroids. The main attraction of this place was a temple located in front of an enormous cave that descended into a measureless abyss, a bottomless pit. The grotto temple was dedicated to the Greek god Pan. The cult worship of this particular god was wild, as in wildly hedonistic and even savage. Locals called the place the gates of Hades with good reason. It was believed to be the entrance to the underworld. Ironically, it is also the source, or headwaters, of the River Jordan. Jesus takes the disciples there, not to preach or teach, not to heal anyone, and not to convert a single soul. He takes them there to ask them two questions. The first question goes like this: "Who do people say that the Son of Man is?" (Mt 16:13).

The disciples have no shortage of answers: "Some say John the Baptist, others say Elijah, still others Jeremiah or one of the prophets" (Mt 16:14).

In other words, there's a lot of confusion out there about who he is. Then Jesus asks the question he's really interested in: "But who do you say that I am?" (Mt 16:15).

Peter replies, "You are the Messiah, the Son of the living God" (Mt 16:16).

This is the first time that any of them gets it right when it comes to understanding who Jesus really is. It's a big moment, and Jesus takes advantage of it to make a big announcement. This is one of the biggest announcements of all time, like God's announcement to Abraham that there is a God; his announcement to Moses that there is a law; his announcement to David that his throne would last forever; or his announcement to Mary that he's sending his son. This announcement is like those announcements; it's that big. He says,

> I say to you, you are Peter, and upon this rock I will build . . .
> —Matthew 16:18

Now hold on, because if you grew up in church, you have heard this so many times; it's easy to not really hear it at all or just take it for granted. You know this, so of course you know he's going to say he's building his. . . . Let's slow down.

If Jesus was going to name the thing that he intends to build, it's reasonable to assume that he would have called it by a traditional name, like "synagogue" or "temple": "Hey guys, what I am going to build is a new temple." But that's not what Matthew tells us he said. Instead, Matthew uses a very interesting word, a word that is not previously found in the New Testament.

He said, "I will build my *church*."

Okay, look at it again.

> I will build my church
> and the gates of the netherworld
> shall not prevail against it.
>
> —Matthew 16:18

Jesus says to the disciples in essence, This is the biggest news of all, the biggest thing ever; going forward, this is the plan, and this is the *whole* plan. For the rest of history, this is what God is going to be doing, and nobody and nothing, not even the gates of Hades (which we just happen to be standing in front of; how cool is that?) will not stop this plan. It's just going to keep growing and going and growing and going. And nothing is going to stop it.

The word Matthew uses is the Greek word, *ekklesia*. But the English word "church" is not a translation of ekklesia. The Greek word was used to describe assemblies or gatherings of people in a given locale, for some specific purpose, usually a civic or community-wide one. Typically it was used in reference to town hall meetings, or the coming together of a city council at city hall for some deliberate purpose that impacts the paroikia (remember parish/neighborhood) and not just the ekklesia. Here's what it did not refer to: a building. On the other hand, the English word "church" derives not from ekklesia but rather from the German word "*kirche*," which is a building.

Father Michael: Sorry. Not trying to show off. I know absolutely no German, and I failed Greek in seminary. I'm just trying to make a point. There has so often been confusion and even conflict over this point that's it's worth emphasizing—Christ promised to build an ekklesia, not a kirche. Jesus was God, so he could do whatever he wanted to do, and he never built a single church; and he never asked anyone else to either. He never spent a minute of his ministry raising money to build or maintain churches. He came to launch an ekklesia.

An ekklesia is a movement. The building project we join him in is not the construction of a building, or the maintenance of a museum; it's not a monument to be viewed or a destination to be visited; it's a movement. So, it has to *move*. And it is a *growing* movement of growing disciples who are gathering more people, who are not disciples, to become disciples.

This is the Church that is so strikingly described in the Acts of the Apostles: a dynamic gathering, a powerful movement with a world-changing mission.

We are indebted to Pastor Andy Stanley at North Point Church in Atlanta for exploring this point in his wonderful book, *Deep and Wide*. While we cannot agree with the whole of his interpretation of Church history, he does point out that, all too quickly in the course of history, churchpeople started to get in the way. Churchpeople so often want to control the ekklesia that Jesus is gathering; we want to contain it in the kirches we build, mostly for ourselves.

- The ekklesia is messy; kirchepeople want to make it neat.
- The ekklesia is unpredictable; kirchepeople want to systematize and codify it and generally make it entirely predictable.
- The ekklesia is a work in progress; kirchepeople want a finished structure; they want a building that houses a well-ordered, stable community. The ekklesia is under construction. It's a building project.

And don't think this is ancient history. It goes on in parishes everywhere, every day. We've done it ourselves for more wasted years than we'd like to admit. On the other hand, when we give building ekklesia a try, it will not be easy.

Ask yourself the following questions:

- Are we making a measurable difference in our community or simply serving our members?

- Are we mobilized for mission or insisting on business as usual?
- Are we here to preserve our broken systems, or are we willing to go where God is blessing?
- Are we simply meeting or are we moving?
- Are we kirche or ekklesia?

If your parish project is building, renovating, refurbishing, or redecorating a kirche, it can be a very commendable, even noble, project. However, this book is largely useless to you in that undertaking. Actually, it will be worse than useless; it will be disruptive to your kirche building project. It will likely make you grumpy, so you should stop reading now.

But if you want to join Christ as he builds his ekklesia (and he is, at this very moment), keep reading; the following tools will help you build better.

STRATEGIC TOOLS

1

DON'T JUST DO SOMETHING, STAND THERE

Be still and know that I am God.

—Psalm 46

If you're working in parish ministry, you probably do too much. There is a lot to do; it must get done; and who else is going to do it?

You have to, right?

> **Father Michael:** I vividly remember a Saturday one spring when I had agreed (reluctantly) to preside at a wedding. I was reluctant because the wedding was at a neighboring parish. The bride, who thought the other church was prettier than our church, wasn't really a parishioner but joined our parish because she needed a priest. The pretty church wouldn't supply one. It was a huge hassle, but I agreed to do it.

That same day, I also had another wedding at my own church, as well as confessions and the evening Mass. I was expected to preach at both weddings, in a warm and personal way, even though I knew neither of the couples very well. And, of course, I had to preach for my weekend Masses.

In the midst of this juggling act, a man I had never met managed to get hold of me to demand (that's how it sounded anyway) that I drop every-thing and come to anoint his elderly father who was actively dying. (Just for the record, his father had already been anointed several times.) This kind of demand is not uncommon. A relative, who has been absent from the situation, shows up at the eleventh hour when there is nothing left for them to "do." Their urgent insistence for the sacrament becomes their contribution to the situation. It's what they do for the dying.

I struggled to imagine how I could fulfill that request and, unbelievably, decided to try. I jumped in my car and took off. Unfortunately, I got lost try-ing to find the address, probably because—like the wedding at the pretty church—it wasn't in my parish.

Eventually I gave up on this wild goose chase, since I risked being late for the wedding, which I nearly was. The bride's mother was freaking out because I was cutting it close on her big day, and as I was on unfamiliar terrain, all did not go very smoothly with the ceremony itself. Nobody there was very happy with me, even though I had done my best.

When I returned home, just in time for confes-sions, the man with the dying father was waiting for me. His father had died in the meanwhile, and he was there to let me have it; and he did, at length. I just stood there and took it; what else could I do, faced with a grieving family member? I missed confessions entirely, much to the chagrin of waiting penitents, and I was so stressed out and shaken up by the time I got to the evening Mass that my homily was largely incoherent. I went home sad, sorry, and spent—and I still had Sunday ahead of me.

Here's the lesson I needed to learn: I did not have to try to do everything I tried to do that day. I could have done less. If I had, what I set out to do could have been done better. You might ask what I could possibly have taken out of that scenario. That's a very good question. The answer probably begins with establishing proper boundaries.

I could, perhaps, have found someone else to do the pretty-church wedding, or to help me out with my obligations back home. I could have told the man demanding the house call that it just wouldn't be happening that day and prayed with him over the telephone. He probably wouldn't have been satisfied with that answer, but at least I wouldn't have been setting up unrealistic expectations and wasting time trying to fill them. I certainly could have carved out more time during the week to prepare properly for my weekend homily, so I wasn't trying to juggle last-minute preparation along with everything else. I absolutely should have set better boundaries and operated more successfully within them.

This is a common mistake among so many people involved in pastoral ministry. Most of us are motivated to help parishioners and be of service to others, and that is surely why we are here. Many of us are also people pleasers; we want to make others happy. This trait will always be a problem, and it is aggravated by the fact that people can be very demanding, especially in churchworld (where the price is right and access is easy).

In our parish, we fell into the same trap. Early on, we developed and hosted myriad activities and programs (in addition to what was already expected). The thinking was that more programs, more events, and more stuff would make our parish more meaningful and have a greater impact in people's lives and in the life of our community.

Perhaps this was most strikingly exhibited each December. We ran around doing a bunch of different activities loaded onto our schedule to "celebrate the season": Breakfast with Santa, Advent Wreath-making, a program we called "Holiday Traditions," and the seemingly inevitable Lessons and Carols. All of these fueled a frenetic pace during an already crazy, busy time of year. In the end, they didn't lead anyone into a growing relationship with Jesus Christ, but it sure did burn us out.

> **Tom:** Some church workers are notorious for keeping up a frenetic pace—always having one more thing to do. We often wear our busyness as a badge of honor; being busy seems to prove our ministry matters.
>
> Sure, there will be busy seasons. There will be days and seasons and special projects that demand we pick up the pace and work harder. But when we spend ourselves in unproductive activities—achieving only fatigue—we are of little use to anyone, and we are not exercising proper self-care. Being busy to the point of distraction or exhaustion certainly does not mean we are living out our mission to make disciples of Jesus Christ.

Jesus was the Savior of the world and yet he consistently kept a sustainable pace, despite demands to do otherwise. One time, he spent the whole day ministering to people of a certain town. When the day ended, there were still more people who wanted to and expected to see him. Sound familiar? Nevertheless, Jesus got up early the next morning and took time to be alone with his heavenly Father. Peter and the other apostles sought him out and asked: What are you doing out here? There are still more people to heal. The whole town is looking for you. But Jesus refused to go back: "Let's go on to the nearby villages that I may preach there also. For this purpose have I come" (Mk 1:38).

Jesus wasn't too busy. He knew enough to withdraw and take personal time to set clear boundaries and conduct his ministry within them. He directed his pace of life, rather than allowing the demands of ministry to do so. He wasn't crazy busy, but he was the most amazingly fruitful, prodigiously productive person in history.

To be less busy and more fruitful (and more effective and successful), we need to be more thoughtful and strategic about what we do. We probably need to do less. Here are some rules we follow in our parish to make that happen.

FOLLOW A SCHEDULE

Make a schedule for yourself each week, share it with the people you work with and care about, and keep it (as closely as you can). At the end of the week, evaluate how well you did: What didn't work? Where were you unrealistic? How could you improve your schedule? Where else can you do less, so you can be more effective in your ministry?

SET BOUNDARIES

Use your schedule to set boundaries. Within the year, where is your vacation time? Take it, and keep it, no matter what. Within the week, where is your day off, your Sabbath? Take it and keep it, no matter what. Within each workday, where is your quiet time, your private time, your prayer time? Take it and keep it, no matter what. When scheduling, also allow enough time between things. Create and maintain margin. Whether you're a priest, religious, or lay minister, you have family and friends as well as a personal life (or at least you should have those things); don't allow ministry to eclipse your relationship with them.

KEEP OBJECTIVE

Do not let the demands, emergencies, or crises of others become *yours*. At least, don't do it often. You will always want to, but don't. It is true that there will be exceptional events in the life of your community and true tragedies that will require you to recalibrate your schedule and your time, but you have to apply your best judgment, not allow others to make that judgment for you. If you have already built margin into your schedule, you'll be able to absorb these events when they do arise. Take a close look at everything you do and decide what you don't have to do, what is beyond your scope, and what someone else could do instead.

After watching the incessant gesticulations of an aspiring young actress, the great playwright and stage director George Bernard Shaw shouted, "Don't just do something, stand there." Sometimes it takes more discipline and dedication just to stand there. Don't just do something; stand there. You have to stop doing stuff in order to pray, think, grow, observe a Sabbath, be still, and know that God is God.

2

AND THEN, FOCUS

[Christ] gave some as apostles, others as prophets, others as evangelists, and others as pastors and teachers, to equip the holy ones for the work of ministry, for the building up of the body of Christ.

—EPHESIANS 4:11–12

A person is a professional, an expert, an excellent craftsman, or an Olympic athlete not simply because of talent. Lots of people have talent. Those who strive for, and perhaps even reach, greatness have something else: focus. Focus is all about clarity and concentration.

If your job is guest services or consumer complaint, then the focus of your job is what is presented to you by telephone calls and foot traffic. If you're a firefighter, you're waiting for a fire. If you're working in an ER, you're all about the next emergency. If you are working in parish ministry, you are not focused on any of those things (at least you shouldn't be). Be careful what you are focused on. Your focus is on ministry for the long haul—keep it there. It won't be easy, but try.

Tom: When I first came to work here, I was the youth minister. I took that to mean I had to create lots of youth activities to get kids to show up and keep them coming back. In order to cover the cost of these activities, I inevitably had to run fundraisers (I didn't have much of a budget). Since the fundraisers were more time consuming and labor intensive than anything else I did, they eventually took my focus off the work of youth ministry. Instead of my ministry, I was doing car raffles, silent auctions, and spaghetti dinners. Ugh! No wonder so many youth ministers get out of ministry at the first possible opportunity. I'll be honest; I seriously considered moving on to find another job, though the sad irony was that I didn't even really know what my real job was.

Anybody who is going to succeed at anything needs focus. The more you have, the more progress you'll make and the further and faster you'll go. When it comes to ministry, the question shouldn't be, What else can I do? The questions should be, What can I do that no one else can do? and What can I do that no one else is doing?

What is the contribution I can make that others cannot or will not make? What can I offer that will make the greatest impact on the overall efforts of the parish's mission? If you are a pastor or associate pastor, the answer is clear: the celebration of the sacraments and the preaching of the Word. Why? Because that is the work no one else is doing: forming the whole congregation in faith for the work of ministry.

If you are a catechetical leader, youth minister, or pastoral life director, perhaps the answer seems less clear, but it need not be; the same lesson applies. If you are in any kind of parish leadership, your focus should be on leading parishioners into ministry and equipping them with the skills and opportunities they need to succeed. You should evaluate everything you do, and are asked to do, through the prism of this priority.

- As a catechetical leader, preparing for and presenting a catechist training session is more important than one-on-one meetings with parents demanding special treatment (e.g., because they missed the sacramental prep meetings you generously offered multiple times, none of which worked for their schedule).
- If you're a youth minster, investing time in potential youth ministry leaders is more important than tracking down the kids who didn't, couldn't, or wouldn't come on the Confirmation retreat. We're not saying that the retreat is unimportant; we're just saying leadership development for your youth ministry is more important to the ministry itself.
- If you're a pastoral associate, there will always be a line of people at your door who insist on meeting with you about their problems, and they will often be the *same people* who talk about the *same problems*. It must be *you* that they talk to because they want your attention (and the price is right). You can do that until you retire; then they'll find free talk therapy somewhere else. Or you can just say no to needy attention seekers and expand your pool of well-trained ministers.

As the apostle Paul instructs us, whoever you are, whatever your position at the parish, your focus should be exactly and nearly exclusively on preparing the people of your parish for the work of ministry, so that the Body of Christ is built up. Your focus is on building.

3

KNOW WHY, WHAT, AND HOW

Go, therefore, and make disciples of all nations, baptizing them in the name of the Father, and of the Son, and of the holy Spirit, teaching them to observe all that I have commanded you.

—Matthew 28:19–20

As churchpeople, we are familiar with religious rules and canon law. Our studies in history and theology help us to know what those rules and laws are, why they're in place, and just exactly what their values are.

Running a local parish means we need to become familiar with something else as well. We need to know our mission, vision, and strategy and then we need to know them better. Mission, vision, and strategy are words we didn't understand when we first began working at the parish. But we've gotten to know them and now know their critical importance.

Mission is *why* we exist. Every parish exists for the same reason. In Matthew 28:19, Jesus said, "Go, therefore, and make disciples." Disciples are students of Jesus Christ. We're in the disciple-making business. That's our *why*. Every parish's mission is the same, but you can say it in different ways. North Point Church, a church in Atlanta we like, expresses it this way: "To lead people into a growing relationship with Jesus Christ." Willow Creek Church in suburban Chicago says it this way: "To turn irreligious people into fully devoted followers of Jesus Christ." And at Nativity we say, "Love God. Love others. Make disciples."

Mission is *why*. Vision is *what*. Vision is a picture of what could be and should be. It is a view of a better or preferred future. Proverbs 29:18 says, "Without a vision the people lose restraint."

Without a vision for our churches and the impact God wants to have through us, bad things can happen—maybe not physically but certainly spiritually. People go off course; they become mixed up and messed up and maybe don't get to know their Savior.

As a church, vision means looking to people we are not reaching but should be. Vision is about solving problems and removing the lids that keep our churches from reaching new people. To only reach the people you're reaching now, just keep doing what you're doing now. But, as Pastor Craig Groeschel says, "To reach people no one else is reaching we need to be doing things no one else is doing." We need to be looking to a future in which we are bringing new people into a relationship with Christ by doing new things.

At the same time, vision is about identifying ways your members should be increasingly transformed by Christ. Vision looks beyond the past and the present. It sees the future and how the future could be and should be better and then rallies people around that preferred future. Vision is about where we should go and inspiring others to want to get there. Vision is about the unique impact a parish thinks it should have.

Ultimately vision is all about—and really only about—God's vision. God has a unique vision for every parish; he has a unique vision for *your* parish, and he'll share it with you if you look for it, and pray and fast for it, too. Your vision is the unique contribution only your parish can make to the movement of the kingdom. While every parish has the same mission, each should have its own, distinctive vision. To lead a local church somewhere specific requires a specific vision.

At Nativity, God has given us a vision to be a church of growing disciples among unchurched Catholics in north Baltimore, who in turn are growing (more) disciples. Included in our vision is the desire to help other Catholic churches do the same elsewhere. Over the years, we have shaped a vision statement, which currently reads,

> Making church matter by growing disciples
> who are growing disciples
> among unchurched Catholics in north Baltimore
> and influencing other churches to do the same.

Mission is *why*. Vision is *what*. Strategy is *how*.

Strategy is how we live out our vision and mission. While it makes little sense to constantly change our strategy in major ways, it must be continually tweaked, modified, and improved. When a strategy is found to no longer work as well as it should or could, it must be completely overhauled or discarded. You need a strategy for getting new people to come to your church. You need a strategy for how to connect those people once they come. You need a strategy to grow people as disciples. Strategy is simply the plan you have to reach people and help them grow in a relationship with Jesus Christ.

When it comes to strategy, we've imitated what we discovered at the largest and most successful churches in the country. Out of 325,000 churches in the United States, only 15,000 are growing churches. That's less than 5 percent. An even smaller percentage of growing churches are intentionally doing so. The rest just happen to find themselves in growing communities. So, it makes sense to pay attention to those churches that are intentionally growing.

We go deeper into detail in our book *Rebuilt*, but the largest, fastest-growing churches in the country all follow some formula that includes the following:

- a focus on the unchurched or dechurched people in our community;
- an excellent weekend experience that relies on good music, a relevant message, and something for kids;
- adult discipleship through small groups;
- members who pray daily, become volunteer ministers, and are growing as givers.

And here's how we apply that into a strategy in our setting.

REACH OUT

Currently, one in three Catholics is no longer connected to the Catholic Church. Our strategy is to reach out creatively to unchurched Catholics in our north Baltimore community with a fresh and relevant presentation of the life-changing message of the Gospel, to make them fully devoted followers of Jesus Christ.

IMPROVE WEEKEND EXPERIENCE

Our weekend experience is central to our strategy, and the weekend message is central to the weekend experience. Music, message, and ministers work together to create an irresistible environment of energy and excellence in which newcomers feel welcome and want to come back. Equally important—strategically—are excellent weekend programs for kids and students where the messages usually parallel the adult message.

REACH UP

Newcomers are invited to come back. Regular weekend attendees are encouraged to take the next step and become a member. Members are challenged to take their next steps: grow in their full and active participation in the Eucharist and the other sacraments, learn to know and love God's Word in scripture, serve in a ministry, join a small group, worship through their tithe or offering, get involved in our missions, spend daily quiet time with God, and increasingly honor God in all areas of their daily lives. Members are also encouraged to invest in and invite their unchurched friends to our weekend experience.

Our strategy is to try to meet people exactly where they are in order to challenge them to change and grow more like Christ. Jesus said to make disciples. That's it. That's what we do. Knowing why, what, and how will make everything else easier.

4

CLEARLY DEFINE EVANGELIZATION

For the Son of Man has come to seek and save what was lost.

—Luke 19:10

One Advent, we decided to host a Breakfast with Santa event. We didn't do it as a fundraiser—at least that would have been a good reason to do it, with a clear and measurable outcome. We weren't that smart. We thought we were doing it as evangelization.

We did a really good job, and after that first year, the event grew. We had delightful decorations, a tasty breakfast efficiently served, games and fun for kids, and a cool Santa. The event grew and grew (and grew) and became quite the enterprise. Great! We proved we knew what Breakfast with Santa was all about. In the process, we also proved we had not a clue what evangelization was all about.

Really, what *were* we doing? We were hosting a feel-good children's event that focused on holiday myths and magic. Where did the Gospel come in? Nowhere. Who were we bringing to Christ? Probably no one.

Who was this event even reaching anyway? No idea. We thought that perhaps people in our community who didn't go to church would be attracted to this program, experience our church as a pleasant place to be, and then come back for weekend Mass, but there was no evidence of that. Our Santa event packed the house on the Saturday before Christmas, but as far as we know, it never had any impact on the subsequent Sunday, or ever. And even if someone had come back to church after Santa, our weekend experience at that point offered nothing for kids, so we would not have been able to follow up effectively. The breakfast was somewhat of a bait and switch.

We did not have a clear definition, not to mention a definite strategy, for evangelization. So we were just out there working hard, hoping for the best. In retrospect, it was simply a fun event for our parishioners' kids and grandkids and an exhausting enterprise for our small staff on the eve of our biggest day of the year.

Evangelization is an overworked word these days, applied to a great variety of church programs and ministries. True, it has both an inward focus of growing disciples, and an outward focus of reaching those who do not know Christ, or need to be reintroduced. It is, however, this latter group that will be overlooked and underserved in our efforts unless effective outreach to them is clearly defined and kept as the number one priority in the parish. To do that, you must clearly define what evangelization (to the unchurched) means. What, specifically, are you going to do about it? How are you keeping track of how well you're doing? Who is doing it?

We no longer do big events like Breakfast with Santa, advertising campaigns, or direct mail appeals. When it comes to evangelization, we go old school all the way.

Evangelization is sharing your faith. So, how do you do it? We begin with a stark and completely simple evangelization strategy we learned from Pastor Andy Stanley: "invest and invite." This is about parishioners being on the lookout for people in their neighborhood, at their kids' school or sports events, or at the pool, people who do not have a church. The idea is to simply invest in these relationships as they happen, and when the appropriate opportunity arises, invite them to church. For us, this strategy is everybody's responsibility. We don't have a committee. The whole parish is the evangelization committee.

Our strategy isn't written in stone, and if we come across a better one, we'll steal it and use it. Meanwhile, the one we've got is simple and clear, and we don't believe that we could possibly keep outreach to the unchurched a priority without it.

How clearly should you define evangelization? As clearly as Jesus did: Seek and save what is lost.

5

PULL DOWN THE SILOS

That they may all be one;
as you, Father, are in me and I in you,
that they also may be in us,
that the world may believe that you sent me.
—John 17:21

As we began to learn more about how the largest and most successful churches in the country operate, we also learned the obvious (yet not so obvious to us) value of great children's programs. At the time, we had a religious education director who ran a religious education program according to the long-established practices for such programs found most places. Beyond that, we didn't know much about it. Anyway, at some point we decided to engage her in an open discussion about what more could be done for our kids, especially on the weekends.

Week after week we approached her with good ideas, new resources, and even attractive opportunities for her to attend seminars or conferences where she could learn about best practices elsewhere. We challenged her to step out of her comfort zone and just try something—anything—new. This she steadfastly refused to do, and week after week, beyond whatever else it was that we brought to the table, when asked what she had to report, she unfailingly answered, and always with a smile, "Nothing new to report."

> **Tom:** What we had not yet come to understand was that our children's ministry was a stand-alone operation, something we eventually came to call a "silo" ministry. Not only that, but the people who were running it, starting with the director herself, wanted it that way. They carefully and jealously guarded their ministry to make sure it remained theirs, and they unerringly resisted any efforts by anyone to bring it into the circle of our overall parish ministry.
>
> This is not an attack on DREs. *All* ministry tends to want to find a silo where it can be on its own, all by itself. We don't know why that is, but we know for sure that it is the drift of all ministry. For example, there are music ministers whose offices are in the church basement because they don't want to run into anybody from the staff, especially the pastor. There are youth ministers who are happy that their youth space is in the old convent, because it's *their* domain, where their stuff is stored, their programs happen, and their friends gather. Likewise, one might find the associate pastor guarding *his* people against the pastoral associate who is trying to poach them to fill holes in *her* program.
>
> For all the current talk of ministry teams, it is very hard to actually field one.

As the Lord called the disciples, he formed them into a cohesive whole, an integrated group, and he always insisted that they work together. The ministry was his; they just got to participate in it for a while. The same should be true for us. The ministry we work in belongs to Christ; we just get to participate in it for a while. We do it together because that's how he asks us to do it and because that's how it works most effectively.

Here's what you can do to pull down silos and move your team forward.

DISCUSS GOALS

Bring people together for mutual discernment of where the ministry, as a whole, is going. Together ask the question, "What are we trying to do?"

FIND CONSENSUS

Come to consensus about the goals. Hold long discussions if you have to, include parish leaders; go to the beach, the mountains, or wherever you need to step aside—but make it happen.

GET STARTED

Then do it! Hold people accountable in the group. Make a disciplined effort that everybody has to sign on to and honor—including, and starting with, the pastor. Keep working at it and praying for it.

Silos weaken ministry efforts, confuse parishioners, and potentially destroy the unity of the parish. Jesus foresaw this danger and that's why he prayed intensely the night before he died for unity among the disciples. It should be part of our prayer, too.

6

YOU (PROBABLY) NEED MORE GRATITUDE AND ENTHUSIASM

We ought to thank God always for you, brothers, as is fitting, because your faith flourishes ever more, and the love of every one of you for one another grows ever greater.

—2 Thessalonians 1:3

Father Michael: I know a priest in another part of the country, a rather dour fellow who speaks in a monotone most of the time. He does his best, but his Masses, and especially his preaching style, are kind of boring, as he himself would readily admit. That is just his style—except for one thing. He is a huge sports fan, and in football season, when his team is playing on a Sunday, he cannot help but talk about it at the end of Mass—that is where all

the reticence slips away, and he becomes a foam-
ing-at-the-mouth, over-the-top, unabashed fan.

Gratitude and enthusiasm are certainly in part a personality thing.
We admit that, when it comes to this topic, we sadly come up short
more often than we should. That said, we want to sing the praises of
this combination of attributes when it comes to your parish ministry because they make everything work better, like lubrication in an
engine. You would be hard pressed to find better attitudes with which
to approach your ministry than gratitude and enthusiasm.

Here are the practical steps for all of us in leadership to take.

BE GRATEFUL AND ENTHUSIASTIC
FOR WHAT GOD HAS DONE FOR US

We must be increasingly grateful and enthusiastic for what God has
done for us in Christ: the salvation won for us and the plan he has for us.

BE GRATEFUL AND ENTHUSIASTIC FOR OUR MINISTRY

We ought to be grateful for our ministry, our calling, for the good part
we get to play in the great work God is accomplishing in our parishes.
We must ask ourselves why our gratitude and enthusiasm is freely
dispensed on everything from electronic devices to food and football,
but when it comes to the work of the local parish church—the most
important work in the world—we are often sadly reserved.

Your people will know if you are grateful and enthusiastic about
what you are doing. Growing in these attitudes will tell them more
about the truth and value of the Gospel message than anything else
you could ever tell them from the pulpit.

BE GRATEFUL AND ENTHUSIASTIC
ABOUT YOUR PARISHIONERS

Let your parishioners and guests know that you are grateful and enthusiastic about them, about their presence at your parish.

St. Paul instructs us that gratitude and thanksgiving are foundational to what our communities are to be. Think about it: Our primary gathering each week is called "Eucharist," which means thanksgiving. We do as our Savior instructed us to do: we give thanks. The whole life of our parish should be a Eucharist.

7

THE NFL IS THE ENEMY OF THE CHURCH

Finally, brothers, whatever is true, whatever is honorable, whatever is just, whatever is pure, whatever is lovely, whatever is gracious, if there is any excellence . . . think about these things.

—Philippians 4:8

Father Michael: Once, one Sunday, I found myself at another parish and was hoping to concelebrate Mass. I met the pastor in the sacristy, and he was more than accommodating; in fact, he encouraged me to take the Mass, celebrate it myself. He had another engagement after Mass (golf) and would have been happy to have a head start. I told him I was very sorry, but I couldn't help him out, because I wasn't prepared. That response seemed to puzzle him.

When Mass got started, the style of the liturgy and preaching was what I would call "loose leaf"—a "make it up as you go along; let's get this over with because we've all got better things to do today anyway" sort of approach. Afterward, the organist stopped by the sacristy for postmortems, which turned out to be a kind of mutual chuckle about how badly things had gone. The pastor remarked, sarcastically, "What do they expect; it's church."

Everybody has had the experience of going to a play, a movie, or a concert and being blown away by the production; we've all dined at a great restaurant where an incredible meal was presented with impeccable service. You can't stop talking about it to friends; you find yourself in sales for it. Think of an experience you've had like that. Now, think about how many times you've had that experience in a church setting.

We are not in competition with other churches; we're competing for a share in people's free time and "disposable" income. That means our competition is the NFL. We know a pastor who likes to say, "The NFL is the enemy of the Church of Christ."

Tom: If you're a football fan, sorry. I am, too, so let me hasten to add: It is not just the NFL. All sports, especially kids' sports in our part of the country, cable TV, whatever Hollywood is currently hyping, and the electronic device of the moment are all among the distractions our culture is providing to effectively keep our parishioners from what should be their primary focus: God.

The point is that we can't take the interest and attention of either our congregation or our community for granted. The only way we know not to do that comes in valuing excellence and working toward it as our goal.

Excellence Honors God

Throughout scripture, we are encouraged to give God our best. In the Book of Psalms, King David exhorts the musicians to employ their highest skill when approaching sacred music. The prophet Malachi demands that the priests and people alike bring their finest offerings to worship. Jesus praises the woman who anoints him with rare and expensive oil. Excellence insists that we always bring our best, because when we do, that honors God.

Excellence Inspires People

It's not about entertainment; it's about impact and inspiration. Excellence will inspire the people in your pews to want to get involved and do more. Excellence attracts people, too. When you create a culture of excellence, people will be drawn to the parish. If, week after week, members of the church have an excellent experience, they will begin to share their experience with others. You won't have to beg people to invite friends, family members, and coworkers to church. You will create an enthusiasm that will create a buzz about your church and lead to invitations.

Excellence Builds Trust

Over the years, we have built up trust with members of our church because they know we do the things we do well. One year, when we announced that we were moving off campus to a new, bigger venue for our Easter Sunday services, we didn't have to sell people on it. This could have been a major controversy in some churches, but not here. Our parishioners went along with us. If truth be told, we were concerned about whether we could even pull it off. The response from the congregation was unambiguous: "We know it will be great. It always is." They had more confidence in us than we did. And because they had confidence in us, they had trust in us and they easily went where we were going.

Here are three practical steps to take.

FOCUS

To value excellence will require you to maintain focus (see chapter 2). Jesus could do all things well; you can't, but you definitely can do some things well, maybe even better than anybody else around you. So do those things. When you spread yourself too thin over too many tasks, then the quality of your work will decline. The same is true of your parish. Spread yourself too thin over too many programs, give your staff and volunteers too many disparate demands, and you will see the quality of your work diminish. Evaluate what you do well now. Start there.

DEDICATE TIME

Excellence requires time and dedication. You simply have to put time into programs and projects to really do them well. You also need time to develop skills necessary to excel. Excellence in preaching takes practice, excellent music takes practice, and excellent teaching, excellent greeting, and excellent pastoral care all take practice.

CELEBRATE WHAT'S WORKING

Honor and reward those who are helping make your programs the best they can be. Promote what you do well as part of who you are as a parish community. Make it part of your brand.

The Bible exhorts us to excellence. That's because excellence honors God, inspires people, builds trust, and rebuilds the Church. Think about those things—a lot.

BUILDING TOOLS

8

SOMETIMES IT'S OKAY NOT TO BE GENEROUS

Well done, my good and faithful servant.
Since you were faithful in small matters,
I will give you great responsibilities.
Come, share your master's joy.

—Matthew 25:21

Tom: I was talking recently with the chief financial officer of a large diocese. He shared with me the experience of meeting with a parish that wanted to undertake an ambitious building program. As the conversation unfolded, it became clear why they needed to build. Over the course of several years, they had allowed outside groups, church-affiliated organizations, and stand-alone ministries to use and eventually lay claim to space on their campus. Now, as they wanted to grow their own ministry, they needed space. So they proposed new space. Essentially, they wanted to raise money from their own parishioners, and take on debt, to build the space they needed because they couldn't use their own space. Huh?

As funny as that sounds, it is a common practice in many churches to lend or rent their facilities to other organizations. We fell for it, too. At one time we allowed a local "single-again" support group to meet in a large meeting area of our building; they were not our parishioners, neither were they really open to new members, so our parishioners could not have participated even if they had wanted to. The single-again people were just an outside group using our building. We let them. It didn't have anything to do with our mission, but it was a nice thing to do for them, although not so nice for the parish organizations that had to schedule around them.

Then it got less nice. When we started reworking our failing youth ministry program, we made the strategic decisions to schedule everything for Sunday afternoons and evenings. Immediately, our little plan came up against the Berlin wall of the single-again group. For a while we actually allowed the situation to stand in the way of building our youth ministry program. How crazy is that?

Unfortunately, it took us a long time, and more than a few unpleasant experiences, to realize that allowing outside organizations to use our building simply wasn't worth it. We did it to be good neighbors, we did it because we didn't know how to say no, and we did it with the hope that eventually they might check out our church on a weekend— an effortless form of evangelization. It just wasn't worth it (because there are no effortless forms of evangelization).

Currently, we have a very handsome café space we use on the weekends as a common area for fellowship. We often receive requests to use it for receptions following funerals, baptisms, and even small weddings. We also get regular inquiries all the time for the availability of our parish hall and even our sanctuary for larger groups and gatherings. Everybody, from community organizers organizing community events to families hosting family reunions, wants free space, or at least really cheap space (which most inquiries are presupposing).

Additional cash would be helpful. Being able to say yes to friends would feel good, especially when these spaces aren't being used on a given day or at a particular time. It can be hard to say no—although it gets easier over time.

It seems right, but letting others use our spaces for their purposes beats up our facility, and always increases maintenance cost. As much as groups promise that they will leave the place as they found it and not get in the way of our staff, they can never live up to that promise. Invariably, it causes extra stress on our staff and serves as a distraction from their real jobs. It also can get in the way of our ministry.

Does it make sense that a perfectly good facility is only used to serve our weekend programs and the programs that support our weekend programs? Absolutely. M&T Bank Stadium, where the Baltimore Ravens play, primarily exists to host eight games a year—ten if you count preseason. Seventy thousand seats exist at a cost of hundreds of millions of dollars, all for a few games a year.

Your parish has an incredibly important mission: to make disciples of Jesus Christ. In your parish boundaries, there's probably nobody else who has that mission. If you don't do it, no one will. You are responsible for using your facility and resources to the best of your ability to advance the mission of the Gospel. That's it.

You can't afford to compromise that mission; you can't be that generous. God will look for an accounting of your stewardship and how well you used what he gave you to advance the movement of his kingdom—not the Boy Scouts, not the rec council, and not the garden club, but his kingdom. Only the good and faithful servant who has enlarged the master's interest can hope to hear the master's commendation to share his joy.

9

DID ANYONE UNLOCK THE FRONT DOOR?

Samuel then slept until morning, when he got up early and opened the doors of the temple of the LORD.

—1 SAMUEL 3:15

You've been looking at your building, your sanctuary, your lobby, your entrance, or whatever you've been living and working in for a long time. Or maybe you've never looked at them closely. Either way, it has perhaps not occurred to you to look at them through the eyes of a newcomer. Even if it has, perhaps they could use another, closer examination. Take a fresh look at your building, or better yet, get an outsider, a trusted friend with an unbiased perspective and an eye for details, to take a look for you or with you.

DOES IT LOOK LIKE IT'S OPEN?

No kidding, this is a legitimate question. Does your campus and building appear to be open and accessible to outsiders? When we first came here, the entrance was neglected and overgrown, and usually chained off, with a small, difficult to read sign directing people to a secondary entrance that was hard to find. The overall effect to a visitor or casual observer was that the place was closed.

We know a new pastor of a church that sits conveniently on a busy road, which is a huge advantage when it comes to evangelization and church growth (theoretically). The parking lot is behind the church, not visible from the road. Parishioners park there, of course, and enter the church through the back door (that faces the parking lot). Over time, the front door, not often used by regulars, remained closed and locked on many Sundays. So, the church looked closed. And, in fact, it was closed, as far as any visitors trying to get in the front door were concerned. Visitors wouldn't know where the insiders' private entrance was, would they?

Think about it. How open and accessible, and for that matter, how vibrant and alive, does your church look? We know a church community with a very old, ugly building. Despite the building, they transformed their facade, the face they show their community, with vibrant, all-weather banners. At minimal cost, they changed their neighborhood's perception of who they are. After that decision, it was obvious they were open for business.

IS IT CLEAR WHERE TO PARK?

In most parishes people bring their cars when they come to church, and if they don't know where to park them, they'll leave. Which door should they use? Is that easy to figure out? It should be.

HOW EASY IS YOUR FACILITY TO NAVIGATE?

Next, ask how easy is your facility to navigate once you're inside the building? We visited a church recently, and there was a clear and logical entrance as you approached the building from the parking lot. But, on entering, we were surprised to find ourselves in the parish hall, not the church. Making our way to the church, unaided by any kind of signage, turned out to be a bit of a trick (we actually ended up in the kitchen). When someone steps into your building, is it clear where they should go?

These are all accessibility issues. And let's face it, evangelization is in no small part about accessibility. Make your parish accessible; make the extra effort. Like the young Samuel, let your first priority be a basic one: Open the temple doors.

10

I'M NOT INTERESTED IN HOW MUCH YOU LOVE JESUS; JUST CLEAN YOUR NURSERY

The LORD God then took the man and settled him in the garden of Eden, to cultivate and care for it.

—GENESIS 2:15

In *Rebuilt,* we told the story of the pastor of a very successful church in one part of the country who was invited (entreated really) to come and serve as a consultant at a church in another part of the country. It seems that this second church was really struggling. They had once been a strong and vibrant congregation that found itself in a cycle of decline, with no end in sight. Generously, the pastor in our story agreed to go. On the appointed day, and just a little early, he arrived at the church. Those he was to meet with weren't there yet, so he waited.

While he waited, he wandered around and ran across the nursery. He walked in.

The first thing he confronted was the odor: The place stunk. The walls were in need of a fresh coat of paint; there were old and broken toys everywhere; the trash cans were overflowing; and there was food on the floor! Everything was deep down dirty, with the kind of dirt that reveals no regular maintenance plan. He thought, "I would never leave my kids in here." With more than a little anger, he turned to leave. As he was leaving, his hosts arrived, greeting him enthusiastically. He told them on the way out, "Here's my consultation. Don't tell me how much you love Jesus; just clean your nursery." (He actually employed a more colorful phrase, but our editor won't let us use it.)

A clean nursery, in and of itself, is not going to grow a healthy parish. But it's a great place to start to do something you can do, whoever you are and regardless of the constraints on your ministry and budget. Dirty ministry space communicates quite a lot, and none of it good. The words that come to mind are disregard, disinterest, and disrespect.

Rigorously cleaning spaces for kids and students will say more about the quality of your children's ministry that anything you could ever preach from the pulpit. They say we care about our kids and ensure that the environments we place them in are clean as well as safe. When we do, we are honoring God.

Clean your children's spaces and then keep them clean—and that won't be easy. Even as we were putting these words to paper, we decided to give ourselves a little reality check. We found that while most of our spaces were clean and neat, one area we encountered actually needed some attention. The goal of clean kids' and student spaces is a labor-intensive one that might have to be micromanaged until your team gets that it's a huge priority for you.

In fact, all of your spaces must be clean. We think three other spaces share top billing and demand your special attention.

NARTHEX

Your lobby, narthex, entryway, or whatever it is that guests walk into when they walk in, makes a powerful impression. Whatever else you do, however much effort, time, and money you put into whatever else you do, will rest on this initial impression.

What are your spaces, especially your lobby space, saying to visitors and first-time guests? Most church lobbies say quite a lot, much of it not good. They are filled with multiple attempts to catch people's attention for various parish activities and fundraisers, all of which are understandable but misplaced.

We visited a beautiful church that actually had an incredibly spacious, well-designed lobby. Probably on opening day, this space served its purpose in an exceptional way—but not anymore. It had become a kind of obstacle course of sign-up tables for various ministries and outreach programs. We compared the experience to freshman orientation at college, with a dozen or so people hawking their deals to newbies. Clearly this church has a vibrant ministry program, and they are working hard at it, with obvious buy-ins from many people. But the expansion of the ministry program is not the purpose of the lobby.

Space permitting, the lobby can be a place for fellowship, where parishioners gather ahead of time and people get to know one another afterwards. Some parishes have even carved out an old space or added a new one to help host coffee or other refreshments after Mass.

But even fellowship is not the primary purpose of the lobby. An entryway, of whatever architectural arrangement and features, is for entrance. The lobby is the place to welcome visitors and guests; it should be all about them, not us. Consequently, if your lobby is trying to say anything beyond "welcome" and, "we're glad you're here," it's probably saying too much.

RESTROOMS

Of almost equal concern are the restrooms; they must be immaculate, and they have to be kept that way all weekend long, which can be a trick.

PEWS

Sharing the top three are the pews, including the pew pockets. What is in your pew pockets; do you even know? If you don't, then we'll make a guess: outdated missalettes, leftover programs from recent weddings and funerals, cough drop wrappers, cough drops, used tissues, and candles from the Easter Vigil. Nobody wants to sit in someone else's trash.

As Genesis describes, care of our environment is ordained by God and honors him.

When it comes to churches, cleanliness really is next to godliness, and it is more important than great architecture (and cheaper). There is simply no excuse for unkempt ministry spaces. You can do this; you just probably can't do it alone. The parishioners need to get involved in ongoing maintenance. A mission of our sister parish in Haiti has a dirt floor in their sanctuary, but that floor and the entire church are carefully swept before every service. Parishioners do the sweeping.

11

CHRISTMAS IS OVER, SO THROW OUT THE DEAD POINSETTIAS

Behold, I make all things new.

—Revelation 21:5

There is one other thing you absolutely need to do when it comes to your facility. You need to get rid of junk. For some reason, churches attract junk. No kidding, this is true. People think every church is their local Salvation Army Outlet. When they clean a closet or the garage, or when they're moving Mom to assisted living and nobody wants to do the dirty deed and throw out what she's been saving and storing for them since kindergarten, they bring it to us. People bring us their junk, and then we can't quite motivate ourselves to get rid of it. After a while, the things almost assume an air of sacramentals.

The problem is only compounded since most churches have plenty of their own junk already. Junk is deep down in the DNA of parishes. There are many reasons why. Nurseries need toys, games are a given for student programs, and how could you possibly do religious education without closets full of supplies, crafts, giveaways, and trinkets? Music programs, regardless of size or quality, will have mountains of music, and church offices are shrines to needless record retention.

Oftentimes churches are on tight budgets, and we are loath to throw anything away because we might need it sometime. This was the prevailing consideration at Nativity.

> **Father Michael:** The first summer I was here, I discovered there was a tremendous amount of space used for storage. The central corridor, in fact, was lined with storage rooms, one after another, all devoted to deep, dense storage with no clear indication of what was being stored.
>
> Being a somewhat compulsive cleaner-organizer, I decided to find out. I started in the pantry, behind the kitchen. As far as I could observe, nobody actually actively used this room. Nevertheless, it was stocked floor to ceiling with stuff. There was so much stuff in there, you had to take stuff out just to get in and see what stuff was there. There were cartons and cartons of foodstuffs, though we served no food that I was aware of. There were freezers with frozen food items under layers of thick ice. There were boxes of old holiday decorations (Christmas garland, lacey Valentine hearts, strings of paper shamrocks, little tiny American flags, and red, white, and blue streamers), all quite tired. There were also shelves and shelves of old dinnerware, some of which had been stored after use without the benefit of cleaning. All of it was dirty. There was ample evidence of pests, too. Anyway, I determined to get rid of everything, just clear it out, and claim this neglected space for Christ and the kingdom.
>
> Two weeks later, a solemn delegation of matrons appeared in my office with fury written on their

faces and fire in their eyes. I had violated the inner sanctum of the Ladies Club, who, back in the day, hosted monthly lunches and teas. The practice had long since been abandoned, as the group aged in place, but it was the fervent hope of the surviving members that the practice would be revived among new generations. Along with that hope, they clung on to the dirty dishes and faded decorations, poignant reminders of the club's glory days.

Now I had robbed them of their legacy as well as any hope of resurrection.

Of course we need to be respectful of others' property and others' needs. That said, there is stuff all around you at your church that you need to get rid of to make room for programmatic space.

It's not inconsequential. It's a problem. If we're supposed to be a movement, how can we move with all this stuff? It's like trying to run a race with lead shoes and a sack of bricks.

Christ promised that he and his Church would be ever new. Can we try to look that way, too? Limp, brownish, dried-up Easter lilies are not a convincing sign of the Resurrection. When the funeral flowers die, let them go. By the way, Christmas is over, so throw out the dead poinsettias.

12

BE A CONTROL FREAK (BUT ONLY ABOUT YOUR BUILDING)

I am telling you this for your own benefit, not to impose a restraint upon you, but for the sake of propriety and adherence to the Lord without distraction.

—1 Corinthians 7:35

Tom: When you go to Camden Yards in Baltimore (and you should, because it is the most awesome ballpark in the world), you can't just do whatever you want to do and go where you feel like going. There are certain house rules governing the experience. The stadium authorities create the environment they want, in part, through your observation of their rules.

You are not allowed to watch the ball game from the dugout or sit in the front row unless you have a ticket for a front-row seat. If the game is in action, the ushers will not allow you to use the aisles because you'll interfere with the experience of other fans. When there is a timeout or a change in batters or innings, then they will let you return to your seat. Until then, you wait. If fans become unruly, calling other fans names or misbehaving in some way that distracts or causes offense, they will be asked to leave. Even though they paid for the seat, their bad behavior will forfeit it.

There are certain rules at Camden Yards about common courtesy that are usually outlined at the beginning of a game. The stadium authorities put rules in place and people in place to enforce those rules because they want their guests to have a good experience. This is true in any almost any public setting; just think about theatres, restaurants, or theme parks.

Most people know how to behave in public environments. Most people have a sense of place and don't come to church to draw attention to themselves. But some people do. People sometimes behave badly; they just do. Without house rules, and without people on hand to enforce the rules, one person's bad behavior can ruin the experience for someone else, perhaps everybody else.

But for some reason, this is not often acknowledged in churches, especially at Mass. People tend to come and go as they like. Mobile phones are a frequent problem, and we're not just talking about the person whose phone rings; we're talking about the person who answers his or her phone. Crying babies and parents who insist on trying to calm them while everyone else is trying to worship are regular features in most places. To be fair, parents are seldom provided any real alternative except leaving the building and abandoning their own attempt to worship.

Father Michael: One recent Sunday, I was preaching, and there was a family in the front row; I could
tell they were churchpeople from some other
church who brought their own church culture with
them and put it on full display. Not once, not twice,
but three times, as I was speaking, the mom got up
to escort, in turn, each of her kids to the bathroom.
They were old enough to go on their own, but
she went with them. Up and down the aisle she
paraded. Of course, all eyes were on her, and she
had to know it. She seemed not at all interested
in what I had to say, nor concerned that others
might be.

Like the people who run Camden Yards, you need to have a plan in
place so that unnecessary disruptions do not sabotage your work and
the mission of your church. Here are the practical steps we rely on in
our effort to maintain control of our building. Still, we admit this is
an ongoing challenge.

SET UP THE RIGHT EXPECTATIONS

We have an announcement at the beginning of Mass in which we
encourage parents with young children to take advantage of our
children's programs (more about these later). If they do not want to
do so, we invite them to sit in one of our video venues (essentially our
"cry" areas) with more flexible seating where children and their parents
can move more freely. When parents choose not to accept either of
these invitations and their children subsequently become noisy or
restless in the main worship space, we will discreetly and politely but
firmly ask them to move to one of the other venues. We soften this
by offering the child a "prize" (a small coloring kit).

Some churches we know do not allow children under five in the
main sanctuary, which is an increasingly attractive alternative for us.

We are not picking on kids or parents with young children. In fact, quite the opposite is true. We value children in our parish and are committed to helping them have a great experience at church. At the same time, we are committed to freeing their parents to have an excellent worship experience. Where in churchworld did we develop the idea that we should force our youngest kids to sit through a service that is incomprehensible to them and why are we surprised when this exercise distracts and often annoys everyone else?

> **Tom:** I am especially amused by the parents who insist on sitting in a front row, on the theory that proximity to the altar will hold their kid's attention. It doesn't, of course, but it very effectively distracts not only the congregation but the celebrant and other ministers of the Mass.

USE SIGNAGE

We post signs throughout the building to assist and guide people on their path through their experience of our church. The signs help people to navigate our building and feel more comfortable doing so. They subtly suggest that we have thought about our building and thought through how they can best use it.

USE VOLUNTEERS

Along with signs, we have volunteer ministers at each step of our guest experience. We have parking ministers in the parking lot to maintain order as well as communicate enthusiasm as people arrive on our campus. We have greeters not only greeting guests in our entry areas but also setting a tone that we are in control of our building. Inside the sanctuary, we have host ministers who seat people, of course, but also help them understand the house rules as needed. By the way, all of these ministers have uniforms and/or name badges, which communicates a sense of order and makes them easily identifiable and accessible.

St. Paul gives a lot of great advice to the Church at Corinth, some of it sublime and some of it quite simple. When it comes to worship, the bottom line for Paul is that the fewer distractions, the better. It's not about rules for rules sake, or being a control freak; it's about creating an environment in which we can lead people to get to know their Savior.

Take control of your building: everyone (well, most everyone) will be glad you did because they'll have a better experience of prayer and worship.

OFFICE TOOLS

13

FOOT TRAFFIC AND PHONE CALLS DO NOT PROVE YOU'RE RELEVANT

We hear that some are conducting themselves among you in a disorderly way, by not keeping busy but minding the business of others. Such people we instruct and urge in the Lord Jesus Christ to work quietly.
                    —2 THESSALONIANS 3:11

Father Michael: When I was a seminarian, I briefly served in a parish one summer that seemed fairly low key, definitely not high energy, except for one thing: The phones rang off the hook all day long. Two secretaries juggled to keep up. At first, it didn't occur to me to question the scenario, but eventually it seemed curious. Why did a parish this size even need one secretary, much less two? What

were all the calls about, and who was calling anyway? Was it a bookie joint?

Here's the thing I learned: The same people were
calling over and over again. They were lonely; they
were bored; and they were conditioned to pick
up the telephone and call the office to get parish
information and personal attention. The same was
true for the foot traffic in the office. It was the same
people day after day, asking the same questions,
indulging in the same small talk, and in this particular parish, gossip.

Foot traffic and phone calls in your office do not prove you're busy,
relevant, or achieving anything really. Sometimes it's all just a distraction from what we should be doing, despite the fact that it's all done
under the guise of pastoral care.

Father Michael: The same holds true for a lot of
"counseling" and office appointments. I know a pastor who came to a new parish and immediately
announced that every Monday his office would be
open and anybody could come and see him for any
reason and take as long as they wanted. Wow, how
I wished I could be that pastoral (not really, but it
sounds good to say so). Guess what happened after
six months? He suspended the practice. The same
people kept coming to him with the same issues
and problems that he could do nothing about and
that they had no intention of doing anything about
either, besides complaining to him.

Cut down on the distractions of the needy who will always be needy, the nosy who will always be nosy, and the nagging who will always be nagging; and, as we mentioned earlier, get focused on what you need to do to be a part of the kingdom movement. Sometimes that means you just work quietly for the Lord Jesus.

14

BREAK UP THE "NESTS"

All who believed were together and had all things in common; they would sell their property and possessions and divide them among all according to each one's need.

—ACTS 2:44

We don't know if it is true in every office, because neither of us has had wide experience (more like no experience), but office space in church-world, spacious or scarce as it might be, seems to encourage "nests." That's what we call cozy corners for staff to hang out and hibernate.

Father Michael: At Nativity, there was once a DRE who took that tendency and raised it to a high art form. Being one of the longest-serving staff members, she had the second biggest office (after the pastor's), and it was quite big—at least, that's what I discovered after we moved her out.

Looking into her office, you literally could not see her because of the piles of junk, boxes of junk, and bookcases of junk. There was a collection of dolls and plush toys and a permanent Christmas display including a small Christmas tree with little blinking lights (she was that kind of gal). You had to gingerly make your way through this maze she had amassed to find her; at the center of the labyrinth she sat, in splendid isolation, doing whatever she wanted to do (which, by the way, was mostly playing solitaire and hanging out on the telephone with her catechist).

As we mentioned earlier, all kinds of staff energy will be directed toward taking whatever ministries staff members are entrusted with and shaping stand-alone, or what we are calling "silo," ministries (see chapter 5). Office nests serve as command centers for such ministries. To pull down the silos, you've got to break up the nests.

Consider, alternatively, the sleek, contemporary office spaces at Apple, Google, CNN, or Facebook; they all have open floor plans. Everyone works together in the same space with adjacent breakout rooms for conferences and calls—no nests and no private space in the team space. The most successful, growing churches in the country that we've visited have the same plan. Hmmm. Maybe there's some connection between their approach to office space and their success.

Take a cue from the Church of the Apostles and rethink your office space. If there is any way to do it, move everyone out of the cubbies, corners, nooks, and crannies they've shaped for themselves and into one central space.

If you can't do that because of the physical limitations of your current space, here's another approach: every once in a while, make everyone move (including you, Father) to a different workspace. They won't thank you for it, but eventually it will strengthen your team.

15

EMPTY YOUR OWN TRASH CAN

For everyone who exalts himself will be humbled, but the one who humbles himself will be exalted.

—Luke 14:11

Father Michael: I was attending a church conference at one of the fastest-growing churches in the country. The Saturday afternoon of the conference, I went to Mass at the local Catholic church. All that weekend, the parish was "celebrating" the opening of "their" new rectory. The congregation wasn't actually invited into the rectory, but the place was described in glowing terms. It was easy to believe the description because from the outside the place looked like a palace. Far from celebratory, the congregation seemed somewhere between disengaged and annoyed.

Jim Collins notes in *Good to Great* (New York: HarperBusiness, 2001) that one of the sure signs of companies headed in the wrong direction is their executive suites. Inevitably, in the failing companies he studied, the suites were too nice, too elaborate, and too big. On the other hand, consider the initial cost-cutting effort from the head of one hugely successful turnaround company:

> He shut the executive dining room and replaced it with a college dorm food-service caterer. He closed the executive elevator, sold the corporate jets . . . he removed free coffee from the executive suite. He eliminated Christmas trees for management.

You get the idea. How does it translate? Well, different ways in different places to be sure, but there is an application here for everyone.

> **Father Michael:** When I came to Nativity, I had a full-time housekeeper. I am not sure there was another person in the parish who had a full-time housekeeper, but I did. Why? Why did I have lunch and dinner served to me every day? Who was I but the pastor of a shrinking parish? The parish was desperately under resourced and understaffed, but I had a housekeeper. What's wrong with that picture? Some places need a housekeeper. I didn't.
>
> Oftentimes there are unexamined features of our ministry that should be examined and probably changed or discarded entirely, if for no other reason than to help us appreciate that the time for business as usual has passed us by (by about four decades). With the exception of historic properties that must be preserved, aren't the days of elaborate rectories and expansive office suites over (not sure when these days started, given Jesus' own instructions to the disciples)? Ought we not, in the face of so many daunting challenges, adapt a humbler,

simpler, and more missional approach to the parish work we do? Would this alone not send a powerful message to our congregations that we're doing things differently?

The amazing example of our new pope, Francis, has already effectively communicated this message in a powerful way. He is humble, as his predecessors were also humble. But Francis is also visibly simple, and his visible simplicity is changing people's hearts. We can follow his example in our parishes.

A good friend of ours is the CEO of a giant retailer, one of the largest, fastest growing, and most successful in the country. One of the lessons we learned from him is that when hiring for his executive team, he always asks himself the question,

"Will this guy empty his own trash can, or does he expect someone else to do it?"

Who empties your trash can? When we are willing to humble ourselves in small tasks, we will see that God will exalt our ministry in big ways.

COMMUNICATION
TOOLS

16

STOP ADVERTISING (OTHER PEOPLE'S STUFF) IN YOUR BULLETIN

Seek first the kingdom of God and his righteousness.

—MATTHEW 6:33

Tom: A parish we know has a bulletin so big it is sometimes referred to as the "in-flight magazine." It is always multiple pages and often holds inserts, too. Why is it so big? For the same reason that your Sunday newspaper is ten times bigger than your Monday paper—advertisements, mostly for other people's stuff.

We understand. We get multiple requests each week to promote other people's bull roasts, bus trips, car raffles, and more in our bulletin. In short,

> we get lots of requests to advertise other people's
> stuff. Many organizations want the attention of
> our congregation for whatever they're selling. It's
> perfectly understandable, since we've attracted
> an audience and other organizations want their
> attention.
>
> But why in the world would we give it to them?
> Aren't we in sales, too? Isn't what we're selling more
> important (eternally more important) than what
> they're selling? You might ask, can't you do both?
> We don't think so, given the slender opportunity
> we have just once a week, at best, to communicate
> with our congregation.

If you have advertisements on the back of your bulletin, because that's how you pay for your bulletin, at least that makes sense and has a purpose. We think it's a poor purpose, but at least the ads do have a purpose. If you're advertising other people's stuff because you want to be a good neighbor and it's simply what's expected, change expectations and be a good neighbor in some other way. If you're advertising other people's stuff just because they asked you to, practice how to politely say no. If you're advertising other people's stuff because you've never considered your communication strategy, start considering it.

When you eliminate all the free advertising you're providing, you might find you can have a smaller bulletin. Or how about this: if you stopped advertising other people's stuff, you might discover you don't even need a bulletin. There's not that much going on in your parish that's different week to week (if there is, please go back and read chapters 1 and 2). That might be a humbling admission but also helpful; doing away with the bulletin will save you time and money.

That was exactly the decision we made, and we don't regret it for a moment. We no longer have a parish bulletin; all news is online. Bulletins, like newspapers, are destined for demise. Put the information that's in your bulletin online and direct your congregation's attention there. That will provide the additional benefit of increasing your online traffic (and you'll have an easy excuse not to advertise other people's stuff).

Jesus himself encourages us to have laser focus on God and his kingdom. It's actually a challenging and difficult thing to do. To get the whole parish focused is exponentially more so. Don't create more competition for yourself, your church, or for the Gospel. Stop advertising other people's events in your bulletin.

17

YOU ARE YOUR WEBSITE

One thing I ask of the LORD; this I seek: To dwell in the LORD's house all the days of my life, to gaze on the LORD's beauty, to visit his temple.

—PSALM 27:4

While your bulletin is old school (and increasingly irrelevant), your website is more important than ever and a greater opportunity than you even realize. The time has come when people will absolutely visit your website before they'll ever visit you, and what they see there will determine what they think about your church. You are your website.

Even more important than a website is a current website, one that is consistently updated. It does not matter at all that you have a fancy, expensive website with all kinds of bells and whistles. It matters incredibly that you have a website and that is **updated weekly**. If you cannot commit to keeping your website current, don't have one. If you have one, keep it current and keep it fresh—add new features and pictures from time to time, and by all means, make it attractive.

Beyond that, decide what your goal is for your website: Who are you trying to reach? If your answer is everyone, everywhere, or you have no idea who it could be, it's probably not going to be very effective.

Here are three things we want our website to be.

A DESTINATION FOR AN INVITATION

The primary focus of our website is the unchurched in our community of north Baltimore. After a personal invitation from a parishioner, our website is our second-most important evangelization tool. In fact, the two go together, because if someone actively considers an invitation to our church, the first thing they're going to do is check out our website. It is the destination for the invitation, so there has got to be information there for them, like what to expect if they do come.

A DESTINATION IN ITSELF

The secondary goal of our site is to make it a destination in itself for visitors to spend time and use our resources. We have the technology to live stream two of our weekend Masses, but we also make available previously recorded homilies and even other talks, like our small-group materials, which we make constantly available to anyone (help yourself).

A DESTINATION FOR PARISHIONERS

Of course, we also want our site to be helpful and useful to our parishioners (they are not our only audience, nor our primary audience, but they are an audience). Our website gives them all the information they need, without needing to call the parish or stop by the office. Our site is an easy, accessible opportunity to sign up for programs, get involved in service and missions, offer comments, ask questions, and donate to our parish.

In the Psalms, David celebrates what he has come to know about the Lord, by spending time with him. Your website can be a place where people in your community who are far from God can get to know you and begin to know him.

It is simply impossible to overestimate the importance of your website. That's why you should spend time on your site, get to know it, and keep it fresh and fun. There are people in your parish who can help you with this (they're probably all in middle school).

18

"LOOK, THEY HAVE A 'KIDZONE' TOO!"

So the LORD God had formed out of the
ground all the wild animals and all the birds
of the air, and he brought them to the man
to see what he would name them; whatever
the man called each living creature
was then its name.

—GENESIS 2:19

When it comes to parish programs in our Catholic culture, we fail to appreciate almost entirely what it is we call things. We simply call youth ministry "youth ministry," the middle school program is called "the middle school program." And, of course, religious education is "religious education" (which is, admittedly, a huge improvement over Confraternity of Christian Doctrine or CCD). We use churchspeak to designate what we're trying to do, in a way that can seem like a foreign language to everybody but insiders—for example, RCIA, Sacraments of Initiation, and Catechetical Formation. What does it all mean?

Who cares? Try making this announcement: Ladies and gentlemen, please join us for an exciting and entertaining evening of Catechetical Formation. You know what kind of response you get to that.

In looking at some of the most successful churches in the country, we discovered that they name and brand all their programs and services with attractive tags that sound like stuff people actually want to do. Here are several great examples:

- "Wamba Land" and "Upstreet" (children's programs)
- "Transit" and "Inside Out" (middle-school programs)
- "2 to 1" (marriage preparation)
- "Thrive" (marriage enrichment)
- "Starting Point" (new member class)
- "Grief Share" (bereavement ministry)
- "Oasis" (single-again ministry)

Everything in our culture is branded. Brand recognition is hugely important; companies invest billions of dollars into it to distinguish themselves in a competitive marketplace. Parishes don't have much, if any, money to invest in branding, but that doesn't mean we can't be creative and resourceful anyway.

At Nativity, we brand everything from RCIA (Vantage Point) to small-group sign-up (Full Circle). We love it and live by it, and now it is an established part of our culture.

So, how do you get started branding your programs?

FIGURE OUT WHICH PROGRAMS YOU WANT TO BRAND

We began in our children's programs because kids love fun names. We named Children's Liturgy of the Word "Time Travelers," the basic focus being that they are going back into the great stories and events of

God's Word. Start anywhere; brainstorm with your team a name you like and brand your program with it.

Don't be afraid to borrow freely from other churches' great ideas. We call our nursery Kidzone, a name we liked and lifted from Saddleback Church. One of our staff was visiting there once and commented with amazement, "Look, they have a Kidzone too!" No, they actually had it first, but that's okay.

PROVIDE TIME TO ADJUST

Tom: Recognize that you will need to grow accustomed to this practice; it takes a long time. Truthfully, it will feel a little weird in the beginning. That's normal. It took some time getting used to my children's names for the first few months after they were born. Their names didn't flow naturally; they felt artificial. But of course, over time, my kids' names just became their names, and it is impossible to think of them with any other name.

Of course, you will have to clarify what you are talking about, in an ongoing way, as part of your overall communication strategy. Our high school program is called Uprising, and every time we refer to it we add a brief explanation, as a tag line, "our high school program." You could even start making the tag line a sales pitch: our kindergarten is called All Stars, and we say, "All Stars. Where every kid is a star."

USE A LOGO

A logo is a mark or emblem used to label a brand. They can be quite simple and are often remarkably successful at promoting brand recognition (think of McDonald's arches or Apple's apple). Find someone in your parish who's artistic and have him or her create a logo that you can use in your bulletin and on your website to give your brand a look.

Genesis tells us that God gave man work to do. Even in paradise, there were jobs. For example, Adam was supposed to guard the garden. Okay, so he wasn't so good at that. But, it seems Adam was quite successful with another job: naming the animals.

From the beginning, God helps us understand that names are important. One of the privileges we have as human beings is the ability to name our children. Sometimes there is a story behind a name or even a whole history. Often they form images or pictures in our minds, they can create accessibility, assist communication, stimulate attention, and generate interest. Branding your programs and services can do much the same things, even forming emotional bonds and building excitement in your parish.

19

CONNECT WITH YOUR COMMUNITY

I hear of the love and the faith you have in the Lord Jesus and for all the holy ones, so that your partnership in the faith may become effective.

—PHILEMON:5–6

Last summer a nearby church announced it was closing. Somebody told us about it, and even though it's in the same neighborhood, we couldn't picture it; we had to drive over and find it. Of course, we'd driven by it hundreds of times; we'd just never noticed it. Apparently the same was true for most everybody else in our community, because the church was closing due to lack of membership and money.

When you are irrelevant in your community, that is one kind of problem. When you are unknown in your community, that is another kind of problem. Nobody is ever going to come to your church if they don't know you're there.

For the larger community in which our parish is located, our church was a no-show, a nonplayer. One of the most common responses we heard from people after we came here was, "I didn't know there was a church back there." We were disconnected to our community, and our attitude revealed that we wanted to remain that way. It was less work. More than that, we didn't really care about the community. Our parish was all about us and our members, and nobody else.

That is no longer true. We are definitely connected to our community; they know we are here. Even if they haven't yet decided to give us a try (or have decided not to), they know we're here.

When we started looking beyond our congregation to our community, the community started to notice us. The watershed event for us was a few years ago when we decided to move off campus on Christmas Eve and into a much larger facility in our community (the Maryland State fairgrounds). That move said to community and congregation alike, we're here for you, whoever you are.

One moving testimony, among many we received that first year, convinced us we were on the right track. A lady shared that she's a nurse and had to work Christmas Eve. That evening driving home to an empty house, she felt a little sad and lonely. When she saw the traffic turning into the fairgrounds, she decided to join us and see if she would be welcome. She was, of course, and that evening changed her life.

We often hear stories like that after Christmas and Easter (which we now also do at the fairgrounds). We're not saying you should move off campus for Christmas; maybe you can't, and it's not about that anyway. It's about getting to know your community and growing in understanding how you can be more focused. Start with this question every Monday morning: If I were a visitor, how would the experience of yesterday's Mass have felt to me?

Connecting with our local community in order to form effective partnerships isn't just about being good neighbors or even about filling the pews. Rather, the Bible tells us that our faith in and love of the Lord Jesus *compel us* to form these relationships.

PEOPLE TOOLS

20

KNOW WHO'S NOT HERE

What man among you having a hundred
sheep and losing one of them would not
leave the ninety-nine in the desert and go
after the lost one until he finds it?

—LUKE 15:4

Connecting with your community is really a question of perspective.
Probably the biggest and best thing you could possibly do for your
parish—the single thing that would affect the most change—has never
even occurred to you. It's all about perspective and changing your
perspective from who's in the pews to who's not in the pews. You need
to know who's not here.

This is difficult because it's hard to stay focused on what you cannot
see. Besides, your members will tend to take up your time and attention. That's the way it has always been.

What we are talking about is a radical reorientation toward out-
wardly focused evangelization, beginning with the pastor and parish

staff, then parish ministry leaders, and eventually including the whole parish. This orientation will strengthen your members' commitments, their willingness to serve and give, and their attitude and spirit. Eventually, it will change the way your parish is a parish. It will change everything for you.

What's the difference? We stopped making it all about the people already in the pews and started making it all about the people who aren't here. This was not an easy change to make. Some of our parishioners passionately resisted this approach and fought us every step of the way, before they eventually got on board. Some others left in search of churches where it can be all about them (which are easy to find). We stuck to our resolve anyway. It was a huge hassle, but eventually many hearts were changed.

Know who's not at your church; who is the quintessential person in your community who doesn't go to church? What is that person like, what does he or she like? What does he look like? What is the colloquial language she speaks? How does he or she spend their time and money? What hopes and fears does that person have? Most critically, what does he or she think about God, faith, and church (if in fact, that person thinks of such things at all)?

When Rick Warren moved to Orange County to start what would become his famous Saddleback Church, he went door-to-door through his community. His first question was "Do you go to church?" If they answered "yes," he thanked them and moved on; if they said "no," he asked them why not and took careful notes. In other words, he got to know who wasn't coming to his church, and with that information he was equipped to build a church that could effectively reach out to them. We're not suggesting you go door-to-door (actually, please don't; unless you're Rick Warren, it could be annoying). But we definitely are suggesting you get to know why the people in your community who aren't going to church aren't going to church.

As we explained in *Rebuilt*, the fellow who's not here in our community of Timonium is Tim, "Timonium Tim" (thanks to Rick Warren for the concept). Tim is a good guy. If you met him at a ball game or a party, the likely places to run into him, you'd like him. He's educated, well-dressed, and successful at what he does. Tim is married with children. He has a beautiful home and a comfortable lifestyle. He drives a really nice car. Tim works hard all week and likes to relax on the weekends. His background in faith is a little shaky; his interest in church is nonexistent. Tim is definitely not in our church. But he needs our church because despite all his affluence and success, Tim's got issues and problems. He needs help, he needs hope, he needs a savior. When it comes to weekend planning, message preparation, and even music selection, Tim is our focus. And we continue to be delighted and amazed every time someone comes to us introducing him or herself saying, "Hi, I'm Tim."

In Luke 15, Jesus tells the parable of the lost sheep. The shepherd knows his sheep, and he makes the lost one his priority. Know the lost sheep in your community and go in search of them. Knowing who is not in your church is about being the leader God has called you to be.

Staying focused on who's not in your pews will initially win you no friends, raise you no money, and get you nowhere. But eventually, it will change everything.

21

VESTMENTS ARE LIKE GOLF CLUBS

What did you go out in the desert to see . . .
someone dressed in fine clothing? Those who
wear fine clothing are in royal palaces.
—Matthew 11:7–8

Some churches have impressive collections of vestments that justifiably serve as a source of parish pride. We know a parish that has a committee of ladies whose ministry it is to sew new vestments and maintain old ones—most impressive.

But vestments are kind of like golf clubs. If you want to spend your time and money on them, that's fine. At the end of the day, however, golf clubs are only useful and interesting to golfers. Vestments are like that; they are only useful and interesting to churchpeople.

Once you start focusing on who is not here, it gives you a different perspective on here. Probably not many lost people are ever going to show up and be impressed with your beautiful vestments, expensive chalice, or elaborate sanctuary furniture—at least if the unchurched people in your community are anything like the ones in ours. Church-people like those things and will often gladly pay for them, but people who are not in church do not. In fact, obvious expense on church stuff is a turn-off for many, if not most, unchurched people.

> **Father Michael:** When I was first ordained, vestments were a high priority for me. I put a lot of thought and time into their selection, and I used a disproportionately large portion of my income to purchase them (in case you don't know, they can be quite expensive). They are still important to me. Though my own taste tends toward the simple, I do appreciate beautiful vestments; I also like neo-classical architecture, renaissance painting, baroque statuary, and polyphonic music. Along with many others, these arts inspire me personally and form a wonderful part of our Catholic heritage that should always be preserved and, in the proper contexts, be promoted. At the same time, they honor God, since he is pleased with beauty (he invented it). But I need to remind myself from time to time that my nice vestments probably aren't going to be breaking new ground for the kingdom here in Timonium.

In Matthew's eleventh chapter, Jesus talks about his cousin John the Baptist. Other than Jesus himself, John was the all-time master of attractional evangelization, but he didn't do it in fancy cloths. Apparently, he was attractive in other ways.

22

CHURCHPEOPLE DON'T BELONG IN THE PEWS

Simon's mother-in-law lay sick with a fever.
They immediately told Jesus about her.
He approached, grasped her hand, and
helped her up. Then the fever left her and she
waited on them.

—MARK 1:30–31

In our first few years here at Nativity, we focused a lot of attention on numbers. A careful count was made at all weekend Masses, and come Monday morning, with equal care, we compared and contrasted those numbers with previous weeks' numbers. Each time the numbers went up, our hearts soared; and each time they went down, our spirits sank. We took those numbers seriously and personally—very personally. We shouldn't have. Week in and week out, attendance numbers tell you next to nothing. We didn't understand that they will fluctuate weekly for myriad reasons that have nothing to do with us. What we should have been looking at were our numbers year-to-year and decade-to-decade, not week-to-week.

Having said that, had you told us we would eventually be making an assertion about getting people *out* of the pews, we would have laughed at you. All our energy was spent in trying to get people *into* the pews and *keeping them there.*

We were half right.

Sure, you want to do everything you can to get people into your church, preferably unchurched people (as opposed to people from other people's churches—don't do that). *But*—once you get somebody in the pew, your goal is not to just keep him or her there until Jesus comes. Your goal should be to help that person grow beyond being a casual consumer of religion through ministry and service.

We don't just want our congregation growing in numbers (more people in the pews); we want our congregation growing in maturity (more members in ministry). We want to be growing wider (more numbers) and deeper (more commitment). We want both. We want every member to be a minister.

That's why we go to a great deal of effort to make nearly all of our ministry opportunities easy and accessible, so everybody can do it. Parishioners worship in the pew and then they get up out of the pew to serve in ministry. Disciples do both.

Here are some other things you can do.

MAKE MINISTRY ACCESSIBLE

We do that by limiting the commitment that people need to make to get started. Initially, we ask people to commit to serving just one time. They can give a specific ministry a try with no obligation to continue. We call it "First Serve" and it's a clear ask. We find that the vast majority of people who try First Serve eventually join a ministry.

MAKE MINISTRY EASY

Many of our volunteer ministries are doing nothing more complex or complicated than pouring coffee and opening doors. Sure, we have more challenging ministries (after all, we do have a middle school program), but usually we invite people to start with something simple.

MAKE MINISTRY PART OF YOUR PARISH CULTURE

To do that, you've got to preach it. When the pastor continually and consistently communicates the importance of serving, churchpeople will get up out of the pews.

> **Father Michael:** Recently, as part of a parish-wide push for new ministers, I said this: "You need to get up out of the pew and start serving. Or, you need to just get up out of the pew and give us your seat back so we can use it for potential disciples."
>
> Yes, there were some empty seats after that, but more than seven hundred people signed up for ministry that day.

The Gospel tells us that one of Jesus' first miracles was healing Peter's mother-in-law. Scripture does not tell us if Peter thanked him for that. The point is that people who encountered Jesus and were healed by him changed; they were different after than before. They started getting involved. Like Peter's mother-in-law, a real encounter with Jesus will lead to service.

WEEKEND TOOLS

23

GREET GUESTS

I was a stranger and you welcomed me.
—MATTHEW 25:35

We both remember attending a conference at an evangelical church in Dallas, Texas. Over the years, we've spent a good deal of time studying healthy growing churches around the country, and this one, Fellowship Church, is one of the biggest. Here's how big it is. Driving there from the airport, the directions indicated that the church is located near a shopping mall. From the highway we could see the mall, but we couldn't find the church. We just kept driving around and around until we realized what we thought was the mall was the church.

Anyway, we were headed into the complex from the parking lot, not paying much attention to anything beyond our own level of discomfort at being in a Protestant setting. That changed when we were welcomed at the door by a pair of greeters. These people weren't merely pleasant or gracious; they were boiling over in their enthusiasm.

Father Michael: I was so taken aback by their greeting that I exited a side door and circled back around, to try it again. Then I decided to try some of the other doors in this sprawling complex. The experience was consistent: They were mighty glad to see us.

I have been around churchworld my whole life, in all different kinds of settings and locations, from St. Peter's in Rome to Our Lady of Perpetual Help on Dogwood Road, near where I grew up. I have never once been greeted with that kind of loving enthusiasm in any of the Catholic churches in my experience. Most often, I haven't been greeted at all. I know there are parishes that do it, but not many, in my experience.

Greet guests and newcomers, not just your friends. Greet the people you've never even seen before. Form a team of parishioners to help you do it, or better still, let the team do it instead of you. There are people in your pews who are better at this than you are. Get them greeting guests.

The Bible addresses hospitality in many places, most compellingly in Jesus' great discourse before his death, as recounted in Matthew's gospel. There he admonishes us that hospitality will be on the short list of our ultimate performance review. Meanwhile, it is a critical ingredient to church health and growth. When people come to church for the first time in a long time (or ever), they are not sure if they are welcome. Dispel all doubt.

24

REMEMBER ALL THAT MONEY YOU SAVED ON VESTMENTS?

But how can they call on him in whom they have not believed? And how can they believe in him of whom they have not heard?

— ROMANS 10:14

Father Michael: When I was in seminary in Rome, I regularly attended a church that was breathtakingly beautiful. It boasted luminous stained glass that filled the soaring interior with almost magical light. The statuary and appointments were exquisite; the maintenance was impeccable. But the sanctuary was so far removed from the congregation that it was hard to see what was going on. The acoustics were such that the Mass was simply inaudible, and of course most Sundays the place was deserted. Maybe these things were not unrelated.

How many times have you been to a church where you couldn't see or hear anything? How many times have people had that experience at your church? Many times? Maybe all the time? Okay, so maybe you can't do much about the seeing part (although we bet you probably can); let's just stick with the hearing part for now. We'll go ahead and make this utterly outrageous assertion (which we really don't think is outrageous at all): The single, most important capital investment you can possibly make in your church is a sound system.

Maybe that strikes you as crazy; maybe it sounds impossible, but it is neither. You are in the communication business, and if people can't hear you, you're out of business (or at least headed in that direction). Nearly any budget can find its way to purchasing some kind of system, even if it's a portable speaker and microphone: anything, as long as people can hear you.

Make the best investment you can make. Remember all that money you saved on vestments? It should come in handy here. The Bible reminds us of a fairly basic, obvious fact that we somehow seem to ignore when it comes to evangelization: How can they believe if they haven't heard?

25

INVEST IN MUSIC

Then Elisha said . . . "Now get me a minstrel."
When the minstrel played, the hand of the
Lord came upon Elisha.

—2 Kings 3:14, 15

Next to air quality and temperature control, music has a greater impact on the environment of your church, at least the emotional environment, than any other single factor. People will walk away from a weekend experience with some impression about your music, and your music will largely, if not entirely, form their impression of your church, perhaps even determining whether they'll consider coming back.

Music has a profound effect on the heart and the soul, an unparalleled emotional impact that shapes not only how people feel about your church but also how they feel in your church about themselves. We may wish it were otherwise and people were more rational, but the reality is that emotions usually provide the greatest motivation for us, especially when it comes to trying something new, like church.

Music is incredibly important. But, as important as it is, it is equally difficult to get right. It seems easy on the surface, but finding good musicians, choosing the right music, and integrating it into the Mass is hard work, especially at first. Moreover, music carries such importance that the evil one will fight us every step of the way. Often it is so difficult that pastors and other parish leaders just give up altogether or manage it into a place where it won't create problems, has little impact on the budget, and is so vanilla that no one notices, much less cares or complains. This is a huge opportunity lost. You need to do better.

Here are some practical steps to invest in your music program.

INVEST PRAYERFULLY

Pray for your music (and fast, too). Pray that God gives you the right musicians who will lead worship, not just song. Pray persistently. We struggled for years (as in years and years) to find the right musicians, as well as the right style of music for our community (which will be different for your community). Without prayer, we never would have found our way.

INVEST FINANCIALLY

While a good sound system is your best capital investment, music is your best operational one. If you're making the kind of investment you should be making, your music budget will have an outsized place in your parish budget. That's good. We hold an annual business meeting where we are transparent about our financials for whoever is interested. Inevitably, year after year, someone will raise concern over the disparity between our music budget and that of other ministries. We understand the sentiment, acknowledge its truth, and keep making the investment.

If you can afford to do it, hire professional musicians, even if you have to cut other things. If, like us not so long ago, you can't do that, find the best talent you've already got in the pew and invest in them relationally; give them help and support to build up your program. Make the difficult decisions you need to make and ask the people who should step down to do so.

INVEST THOUGHTFULLY

Careful thought needs to be given to how the music is heard by your target audience, especially the unchurched. Catholic churches tend to play church music for churchpeople. But what kind of music do the people in your community who aren't going to church like? How does that translate into the sacred music or worship music in your setting?

At Nativity, we are trying to reach Timonium Tim, the guy in our community who hasn't been to church in a long time. We want Tim to feel comfortable with our music, and Tim isn't listening to organ music in his car on the way to work. Oddly enough, that came as a huge revelation to us. It took us a long time to move beyond the music we like and want to a style that Tim finds attractive.

We're not suggesting any particular style of music, but we are strongly advising that you give a lot of thought to the kind of music that is going to connect with your community.

Music and singing play a tremendously important role in the life of God's people. Over and over again, Psalms exhort us to sing, and that is what the faithful and the grateful did, from Israel's Exodus to Jesus' Last Supper. In the Book of Kings, we read that music in service to God can be grace filled and powerfully transformative for a community, but it doesn't always come naturally to us; we need all the help we can get. Get it.

26

NOBODY IS GROWING IN CHRIST JUST BECAUSE OF YOUR PIOUS PROCESSION OF ONE

All you people, clap your hands;
Shout to God with joyful cries.

—Psalm 47:2

Father Michael: I helped out at a church one summer where someone had very effectively trained the lectors to take their good old time. These people didn't just read slowly; they were slow to get started. The sanctuary was huge for starters, and the lectors sat on the opposite side of the sanctuary from where they read. When the time came, they would rise from their place, process across the altar, pause in the middle and bow, continue to the lectern, pause again, bow again, inevitably read-just the microphone (which they could have done ahead of time, had they wanted to), and finally read the reading (which was sometimes shorter than the ritual leading up to it). Next, the whole process was inverted as they returned to their seats. Only after they were all the way back where they started did the cantor take her turn. Just as everyone was suspecting (and dreading) she had the same choreography, only this was worse, because we knew it was coming. And we still had the second reading and gospel to go. It was like a slow-motion ballet without the music.

The Eucharistic ministers at this place had similar, time-consuming rituals. Their movement to and through the sanctuary was so needlessly elaborate that we came to call it "the dance of the seven veils." It was beyond precious; it was mind-numbing. Nobody was growing in Christ just because of these pious processions.

When unchurched people come to church, their number one question (at least initially) is, how long is this going to take? It doesn't actually matter how long it really takes; it only matters how long it *seems* to take. If they don't know how long it takes, and it looks as if it might take a long time, or it feels as if it's going to take a long time, they are going to be very uncomfortable.

We like to stay as far away from liturgical issues as possible; it's safer that way. Plus, we don't know what we're talking about when it comes to liturgy anyway. By all means, Mass should be celebrated with all possible reverence and dignity that includes good pacing, measured pauses, moments of silence, and solemnity.

But can we just ask one simple question? What is the deal about everything at Mass going so slow that it hurts? Mass does not have to hurt. Think about these practical steps.

LOOK AT YOUR LECTORS

Is everything they're doing helping to focus on God's Word, or is it distracting people and drawing attention to themselves? An overdone procession to the podium is of no value to the liturgy or the congregation.

LOOK AT YOUR EUCHARISTIC MINISTERS

Do they have time-consuming, mostly made-up rituals that prevent them from performing their ministry in an efficient manner? Are they presenting themselves as humble servants or the privileged few?

LOOK AT YOUR ALTAR SERVERS

Are they properly and thoroughly trained to blend into the background and serve, or are they an annoyance and a distraction? By the way, we personally think this is a perfect ministry for high school boys (but that's another book).

"Saying" Mass is a public presentation, and in order to not be boring, it must have texture and flow; there should be a pacing to it that suggests someone responsible is in charge of this enterprise and it has a beginning, a middle, and most definitely an end.

Ask yourself this one, simple question: Is anybody shouting for joy at the end of your celebration? If they are, is it because the liturgy was filled with joy or is it just because it is finally over?

27

MANAGE THE TRANSITIONS

You shall blow the ram's horn and cry, "Long live King Solomon!" When you come back up with him, he is to go in and sit upon my throne. It is he that shall be king in my place.

—1 KINGS 1:34–35

Father Michael: A while back, we had an extremely talented music director, and one year, on the feast of Christ the King, he decided he wanted to introduce the weekend liturgies with a specially assembled choir to offer Handel's epic anthem "Zadok the Priest." If you are unfamiliar with this piece, it is a splendidly grand confection of a composition that is actually used for royal coronations (no kidding). Argue, if you care to, about the liturgical suitability of this piece, but it was stunning. Overwhelming really.

With mighty fanfare and tremendous flourish, the choir lavished this anthem upon us, eventually coming to the thunderous conclusion, "God save the King, God save the King. Alleluia, Amen, Amen, Alleluia, Amen, Amen, Ah, Ah, Ah, Ah, AMEN!"

Whereupon the presider, a regular weekend helper, who had an uncommonly annoying sharp sort of voice, followed up this massive musical introduction as follows: "There's a powder blue Cadillac in the parking lot, license plate AZT 511. Your lights are on."

The choir director almost quit that night. He appeared moments later in my office. "Uh, aren't you supposed to be doing Mass?" I asked. He screamed, "I will not work in this toxic environment." Of course, he overreacted (imagine that), but he was right. The moment was lost. The presider squashed it and made it clear who was really in control.

In addition to the things that make up your weekend experience, think about the things in between those things. How do they sit together; what do they say to one another and about one another?

Tom: I remember a Christmas Eve service in which the celebrant gave a very moving homily. It definitely created a "moment" that I am sure touched many people's hearts, and it could have made a powerful transition into the Liturgy of the Eucharist. But it was not to be: Immediately following this beautiful moment came a less beautiful one, far less beautiful. The pastor stepped in to give a stern admonishment on the importance of the Christmas collection for the parish to achieve its budget.

Father Michael: I had a funeral recently for a lovely lady who died way too young. Her funeral Mass was simply transformative. It did exactly what funeral liturgies done well can do. The liturgy soared to spiritual and emotional heights through communion and beyond into a heartachingly thoughtful and loving eulogy given by her son. By the time the prayers of commendation were complete, there wasn't a dry eye in the house. It was a moment that honored the deceased, helped everyone grieve, and brought hope. Then the funeral director shattered it completely with unnecessarily detailed directions to the luncheon.

Think about this: What is the experience of your guests as they enter your campus and find a parking spot? What does the transition from outside to inside look and feel like? From lobby to sanctuary? What kind of atmosphere are you trying to achieve as someone sits in his or her seat before Mass? Are you trying to achieve anything at all? The transitions during Mass need special attention and the cooperation of different people, from the Opening Rite through the Liturgy of the Word; from the Offertory, to the Closing Prayer. These can all be places where you lose people, confuse them, or just erode what you've already accomplished. Plan them instead, and rehearse them carefully until they become second nature.

King David took great care with the transition to his successor, down to the finest details. It was wonderfully successful, though sadly one of the very few in the history of Israel. Many of the others involved conflict, even war. Transitions are important, and if we don't handle them well, there may not be bloodshed, but it can be ugly. Start taking a look at the transitions within your celebration of the liturgy.

That easily brings us to the next point.

28

TAKE PEOPLE ON A JOURNEY

Now that very day two of them were going to a village seven miles from Jerusalem called Emmaus, and they were conversing about all the things that had occurred. And it happened that while they were conversing and debating, Jesus walked with them.

—Luke 24:13–15

As a church, we have the job of leading people into a growing relationship with Jesus Christ. A *growing* relationship means that none of us has arrived. None of us is where we could be and should be in our relationship with the Lord. We have potential for more: we can love God more; we can love one another more; we can be growing as kinder, more patient, and more generous people; and we can be helping other people to do the same.

Whether it is the weekend homily, student programs, kid's stuff, or whatever we're doing, spiritual leadership requires that we move people from where they are closer to where they need to be. We want to move the unchurched beyond a secular or selfish worldview closer to Christ, and we want to move churchpeople beyond comfortable consumerism, closer to Christ, too. That means that we need to take people on a journey.

When it comes to the weekend experience, this essentially requires three steps.

INVITATION

To take people on a journey, we need a place to start. This means inviting people in and providing a warm welcome for newcomers and a warm welcome back for regulars. It also means we put time and effort into understanding where people in our pews are intellectually and emotionally, connecting to their heads and their hearts from the start.

TRANSPORTATION

To take people on a journey, we need transportation. For mature disciples, this will be the celebration of the Eucharist itself. For the unchurched, that is not the case; they do not understand what the Eucharist is so it may not move them anywhere. But music will. We like to say that music is the water on which the entire weekend experience sails (or sinks).

DESTINATION

To take people on a journey, we need a destination. How do we want the journey to end? How do they feel when they leave? What is it they will go and do as a result of this experience? What is different after than it was before?

In Luke 24, Jesus joins two of his disciples on a trip to a place called Emmaus. It becomes, however, a very different journey than the one they had planned, as he leads them from confusion to understanding, from doubt to faith, and from fear and isolation to the very heart of the Church, the Eucharist itself. Spiritual leadership is always about taking people on that journey.

29

KNOW WHAT SEASON YOU'RE IN

There is an appointed time for everything,
and a time for every affair under the heavens.
—Ecclesiastes 3:1

It is interesting to us, as we have studied successful evangelical churches across the country, to find them increasingly referring to and even planning around Lent, Advent, Ash Wednesday, Good Friday, and Palm Sunday. This was not previously the case and seems to us a positive, perhaps important, development for Christian unity.

As Catholics, we enjoy the benefit of the liturgy's seasons and the lectionary's cycles. It is definitely an advantage to be able to rely on the liturgical year, week after week, and shape weekend homilies around it, as well as provide the appropriate seasonal music.

But, while the liturgical seasons resonate with us insider churchpeople, they do not necessarily do so with the average parishioner, much less the unchurched person who might be coming through your front door for the first time. However, they are living in cultural seasons that, to some degree, parallel or at least complement the seasons of the Church's year (as some of our evangelical friends have figured out). Your church and your weekend experience need to be in sync with those seasons because they shape where the people in the pews are emotionally and also intellectually.

The culture where you serve might be different, so let us make the disclaimer that we are talking about an East Coast, mid-Atlantic, middle-class kind of culture. Here in Timonium, Maryland, the seasons pretty much run as follows:

- *Back to School* (Labor Day weekend through the weekend before Thanksgiving): This is the "new year" in our culture; everyone returns to regular schedules, school starts, kids' sports programs get underway (soccer and football), and the NFL is back on Sundays. Halloween is a huge deal for families with little kids and for young adults. It's the usual time to get kids and students into our programs, and we see a big bump in Mass attendance.
- *Christmas* (The weekend after Thanksgiving through Christmas Eve): More kids' sports programs get in the way of everything else (basketball, hockey, and indoor soccer). Schedules are more than overflowing with shopping, decorating, entertaining, and travel. And yet, this is a season in which people are interested in coming to church and very likely to invite unchurched friends to come with them. Our attendance will continue to climb here, and we can definitely expect increased giving.
- *Winter/Early Spring* (The weekend following New Year's Day through the fifth Sunday of Lent): The kids' sports that started before Christmas are still going strong. This season is marked by Super Bowl, Valentine's Day, and St. Patrick's Day, and (in our community) at least one long weekend away at some point for sun or skiing. This is usually a good time of year to sign people up for ministry and small groups. It seems people are more willing to

listen, get involved, and try new things during this period. We have come to call this period, "our time."

- *Spring/Late Spring* (Palm Sunday through the weekend before Memorial Day): Easter and Mother's Day, of course, are the big days (for brunch), and more kids' sports programs are blossoming (lacrosse and baseball). This is a time of transitions: First Communions, Confirmations, graduations, and weddings. This is the season to sign up volunteers for the fall.

- *Summer* (Memorial Day weekend through the weekend before Labor Day): This is a time marked by Father's Day (not nearly as important as Mother's Day), July 4th, and, especially in July, pervasive summer vacations. During this season, we can expect to see weekend attendance drop by a third or more, but this is also a time when people who are church shopping often go shopping. There is a very relaxed feel that settles over our community; people come to church dressed very casually. For our staff, this is the season of preparation for the year ahead. Any capital improvements on campus happen now too.

Those might not be the seasons in which your congregation lives, but your members definitely live their lives in cultural seasons. You should know your congregation's seasons, and those seasons should be reflected in your weekend homily and music. These seasons might determine other elements of the experience as well (like altar decorations or after-Mass fellowship).

Father Michael: So, among other things, distinct seasons means I am not going to give the same challenging message that people might be expecting in Lent on a summer weekend when everybody is headed to the pool. I am probably going to be more inspirational in December and more motivational in September. I am not taking vacation before

Christmas or during Lent. I am not trying to raise money in August.

Besides the macro-seasons brought to us by the calendar and the culture, there are also mini-seasons of life in our community, brought to us by events or circumstances. If you want to be relevant and effective in your community, you have to understand that and be on the lookout for them.

I remember hearing about the shooting tragedy in Newtown, Connecticut, on a Friday afternoon. Instantly, I knew in my heart that what I had planned to say on Sunday was no longer appropriate because it was no longer relevant to where the congregation would be emotionally. I did not want to throw away a week's worth of hard work on message preparation, and I didn't want to try to pull together an entirely different message on the fly, but I knew I had to. I had to address what had happened. And, just as I expected, huge crowds of people came out on Sunday, and they were clearly waiting for, well, they didn't even know what they were waiting for, but they were waiting for me to say something. They wanted me to sort it out for them and place their pain in the context of faith. Besides the new homily, we toned down the music and gave the whole weekend a more somber feel.

Scripture says there is a season for everything, a proper time for everything under heaven. Doing more successful ministry means knowing which season you're currently in or which season current events have unexpectedly created for you. Know and honor those seasons.

When we get this right, it's a big win and moves us a lot further down the road of being a useful part of people's lives. You can almost hear people thinking, "Yeah, my parish gets it!"

PREACHING TOOLS

30

FIND YOUR MESSAGE; THEN STAY ON IT

Always be ready to give an explanation to anyone who asks you for a reason for your hope.

—1 Peter 3:15

Tom: One weekend we had several special announcements that we needed to communicate. Michael mentioned one of them in his homily, but not in a way that I liked. I was scheduled to step in after communion and make two of the other announcements, which I did, but not in a way Michael liked. After I was finished he, in turn, restated my announcements his own way and then returned to his original announcement, just for good measure. We walked away annoyed and irritated with one another. Worse still, we're sure the average person in the pew had absolutely no conception about what our message was.

The problem for some preachers and church staffs is that they have no message. They communicate endlessly, but they just have nothing to say, at least nothing that anybody cares about or anything Jesus told us to say. That's one kind of communication problem. Here's another: You have a great message, a relevant message, an impactful message, and a God-honoring message. In other words, you've found your message; you just can't stay on it. That's a problem for sure.

Your homily and your pulpit announcements should form a consistent message that preachers and parish staff have all bought into. And then, like a good candidate in a winning campaign, your parish team has to stay on message. That is a deliberate discipline, meaning it takes work. You can't just get up to preach the homily or make the announcements and shoot from the hip, saying whatever you want.

When it comes to the homily (which we've actually come to call the "message"), it all comes down to two fundamental questions that we have adopted from Pastor Andy Stanley: What do you want them to know? What do you want them to do?

Do you have a message? Prove it: Can you say it in a single sentence? In one sentence can you tell your congregation what you want them to know and what you want them to do? Look at the following examples.

> What do you want them to know? *God wants you to trust him.*
>
> What do you want them to do? *Spend six minutes a day in the coming week in quiet time/prayer time to demonstrate and strengthen your trust.*
>
> What do you want them to know? *Hurt people hurt people, but God wants to heal us and make us whole.*

What do you want them to do? *This week, every time you find yourself getting anxious, angry, or upset, stop and pray for God's healing help.*

What do you want them to know? *Prepare the way of the Lord this Advent season.*

What do you want them to do? *Get rid of some of the noise in your life this holiday season: less TV, technology, and texting.*

That's it; it's got to be that simple or it's too complicated.

Although it is one of the shortest books of the Bible, 1 Peter has a lot of valuable insight into the Christian life. This little letter forms a message that is both sublime and practical. Peter tells us that he writes to instruct and to encourage (5:12). When it comes to your message, always be ready to give an explanation of what you're trying to do.

31

ONE CHURCH, ONE MESSAGE

Death and life are in the power of the tongue.
—Proverbs 18:21

When we first came here, there were four regular weekend assistants who shared the pulpit. One guy was a very laid-back, easy-going kind of fellow who spoke in the velvety smooth voice of a radio announcer. The next guy was a bit dramatic and theatrical; he liked props, tricks, and stunts. The third guy was a college professor, and he tended to teach when he preached. The fourth—well, the fourth was a "get it over with" kind of preacher. None of them were bad; in fact, they all had their strengths, and each had his own followers and fans. The laid-back guy could be extremely comforting and pastoral; the entertainer was very entertaining; the professor struck many people as interesting and instructive; and even the "get it over with" guy could turn a clever phrase and sometimes be quite funny.

Father Michael: A lot of people might have looked at my situation and envied me for all the help I had. I was happy to have it. It took me a long time to realize I had too much help.

Four different preachers (in addition to me) guaranteed that members of the parish would not hear the same message on the weekend. Sometimes it meant they would receive conflicting and even contradictory messages.

In addition, and much more consequentially, week after week, I was just giving away my very best shot at communicating to my congregation. The average parishioner only heard me, at most, once a month. This limited my ability to build a relationship with them as well as grow in my own skill at preaching. But there was a bigger miss going on.

As we studied healthy, growing churches, we discovered they all always have a single message or homily throughout the weekend. Why? Everyone in these churches hears the same thing, which, among other values, has the added value of keeping everyone moving in the same direction, increasingly aligned around a common mission and vision.

Father Michael: The decision to take control of my pulpit, offering one message for the whole church, has had a major impact on the good and growth of our community. It is no exaggeration at all to say it has affected every area of parish life: increased giving, expanded ministry, growth in our missions program, greater use of the Sacrament of Penance, and increased Mass attendance; the list goes on and on.

Preaching shapes the culture and the conversation of a parish. If the preaching is solidly rooted in God's Word and strives toward excellence, it will shape the culture in a healthy way and the conversation will help bring about conversion. More simply stated, good preaching leads to life change. If the preaching is poor, or just uneven, the conversations that take place in the parish are often unhelpful or even hostile to life change, and the culture will languish.

Preaching is critical. It shapes your parish. And that is why it is so sad that all too often pastors take a pass on the power of their pulpit. Until you take control of your pulpit, you will not see consistent growth and life change, and you will not be achieving your parish's real potential.

Here are some practical things to do.

COMMIT TO HAVING THE SAME MESSAGE ALL WEEKEND LONG

No matter who the celebrant is, the same preacher can step into the pulpit when it is time to preach the homily. If you have an associate, a weekend assistant, or a deacon, you can trade off weekends and take turns (which would actually reduce your current workload). On the weekends you are preaching, try to keep your other commitments to a minimum; make your preaching your priority. Speaking three or four times on the same day is exhausting (especially the first few times you do it), so you'll want to conserve your strength.

MAKE YOUR HOMILY A GREATER PRIORITY IN YOUR WORKWEEK

In fact, after the celebration of the sacraments and the essential pastoral care you need to provide, prioritize homily preparation above everything else. Set aside time in your schedule for it, and don't let anything or anyone interfere with that time. Two hours of preparation is not enough; four hours is not enough; and if you're not very good at writing and speaking, eight hours might not be enough. You need to set aside significant time in your week for homily preparation.

As part of your preparation, "test drive" your message in front of staff or parishioners. On big weekends such as Stewardship Sunday, invite input from key leaders or on special occasions (such as Christmas and Easter), invite actual unchurched people to the preview (you'll be surprised to find they'll be flattered by the invitation and open to participating). Get their feedback and then go back and incorporate it into your message.

CONTINUE LEARNING

Learn more about message preparation and the importance of the message in our book *Rebuilt*. You can find the information in chapter 9, "Make the Message Matter." But don't stop there, because we don't know everything; a wealth of great resources is available online, most of it free. Make it part of what you do as a speaker to be researching what's out there. Especially take time to listen to or watch great preachers, regardless of denomination. Be on the lookout for the guys who have a style that is compatible with your style. Learn from them.

You have to hold on to your pulpit, or wrestle it back from whomever you've given it away to, because even though preaching at times feels unproductive, the reality is that words are powerful. The Bible says they have the power of life and death. That's real power. Use that power; don't give it away.

32

COMFORT OUTSIDERS/ CHALLENGE INSIDERS

They went away one by one, beginning with the elders. So he was left alone with the woman before him. Then Jesus straightened up and asked her, "Woman, where are they? Has no one condemned you?" She replied, "No one, sir." Then Jesus said, "Neither do I condemn you."

—John 8:9–11

Woe to you, scribes and Pharisees, you hypocrites.

—Matthew 23:13

Imagine that you decide to dine at a new restaurant for the first time. As your evening unfolds, you gradually discover things are not what you had expected. For starters, there's a dress code: jacket and tie are required. You have to eat your food in a certain order, with prescribed courses. The menu uses strange words and phrases to describe the food in a way that you largely don't understand. What you do order turns out to be not at all what you thought; it's unappetizing, even distasteful.

The maître d' is condescending, the waiter is slow, and the other guests are unfriendly in a way that makes you feel uncomfortable (as if they're somehow different than you). Worst of all, while making the rounds to flatter and fawn over the regulars, the chef inadvertently insults you; you can hear him making fun of people (like you) who don't appreciate his food. The regulars glare at your kids. Clearly there is nothing here for children. Finally, another couple shows up to tell you that you're actually sitting at their table.

How soon would you go back there? How quickly would you find other things to do? And how much like that experience is the experience of our parish for the unchurched? Maybe more than a little.

So often our churches and the message of our preaching reflect that crazy restaurant. If new people do find their way to us, how we treat them, and especially what we say to them, is often not helpful. Sometimes it can be worse than that; it can be insulting. It can turn them off and send them away, sometimes for good.

On the other hand, we speak very differently, very carefully, to insiders. We comfort the insiders by saying exactly what they want to hear, what they expect to hear, and what they've heard a thousand times before. We boldly affirm truths they already have and hold, and then we let them off the hook with the ones they don't really care for.

We challenge outsiders to accept the world as we see it, and we comfort insiders with affirmation of the world as they want it. As a result, our congregations drift into irrelevance. If you want to grow a healthy church community, you've got to turn that around.

CHALLENGE INSIDERS

Challenge insiders in the ways they need to hear, so that they can keep growing as disciples. We like to talk about this as "taking their next steps": giving (money and time), growing (in prayer, God's word, and the Eucharist), and volunteering (in ministry). The basic challenge is to grow as a disciple, and when members are growing as disciples, guess what? It's more attractive to the unchurched.

COMFORT OUTSIDERS

Comfort outsiders by first of all speaking to them as if they're actually there, even if they're not (they never will be unless and until you start talking to them). Your basic message to them is, "Relax, none of this applies to you." They always get a free pass when it comes to any kind of challenge, beyond the challenge they've already met (showing up). Make sure you thank them for showing up, in front of the whole congregation.

CONTINUE DISTINGUISHING
BETWEEN INSIDERS AND OUTSIDERS

Keep making this distinction in all of your preaching and teaching, and even in your announcements.

Jesus was very clear about this throughout his ministry. The people he consistently challenged were the churchpeople, the religious leaders of the day. With them he could be quite stern. On the other hand, he was nothing but loving to the lost he encountered. He just wanted to find them and help them get to know him better. Could we be more like that in our parishes?

33

PREACH THE ANNOUNCEMENTS

Now when they heard this, they were cut to the heart, and they asked Peter and the other apostles, "What are we to do, my brothers?" Peter said to them, "Repent and be baptized . . ." and about three thousand persons were added that day.

—Acts 2:37–38, 41

A parish is in the communication business. As we have already noted, that seems an excessively obvious, yet widely overlooked, fact. We need to communicate the "Good News" of the kingdom of God. We need to communicate God's Word and how its application can change people's lives. We need to communicate the unparalleled value of the Eucharist as life-changing communion. We need to communicate the steps to take to make that application and get involved in that kingdom.

More than ever, communication is challenging. People have all kinds of information coming at them all the time. Our parishioners are overwhelmed with information and communication. We're in a difficult business. We have to be deliberate and strategic and work hard at it.

Most parishes already have various instruments for communication: the bulletin, bulletin boards, announcements after Mass, posters in the lobby, the sign out front, and, of course, the parish website. However, they all pale in comparison to the pulpit.

The pulpit, the weekend message, is the rudder of your church ship. Wherever the preaching goes on a consistent basis, the church will move in that direction. Whatever the pastor promotes from the pulpit takes on added weight (sometimes, in amazingly effective ways).

Use the authority and power of the pulpit to effectively and successfully communicate your "announcements," but don't waste that authority on announcing bake sales and bus trips. We are not talking about those kinds of announcements. We're talking about the really important ones. The ones that will change your parish: the announcement of the kingdom of God and the invitation to become a disciple.

Here are three practical announcements you should be communicating.

PREACH DISCIPLESHIP

We're talking about announcing what discipleship looks like in people's lives, the habits they need to form as disciples.

Preach the necessity of daily quiet time, weekly worship at Mass, the necessity of ministry and missions, the value of giving and tithing, small groups, and increased use of the Sacrament of Penance. Preach those announcements.

Don't try to tackle the whole of discipleship every weekend. From time to time, devote the entire weekend message to ministry, missions, small groups, giving/tithing, or Confession. We'll even be upfront about it, saying, for instance, "The purpose of this message is to convince you to volunteer in ministry."

On the other hand, you can be peppering your message with encouragement for their discipleship all the time. So, if we're talking about relationships, we might say (in an offhanded way), "Your need for relationships, by the way, is why we encourage small groups." If we're talking about sin, we might say, "Confessions are next Saturday from 1:00 to 3:00 p.m."

PREACH STEPS

Give them specific steps to take on their path to cultivating those habits. If you're talking about daily quiet time, point them to resources they can use to help make it happen. If you're talking about small groups, give them a specific opportunity to sign up and get involved. If you're talking about getting into mission or ministry service, tell them when, where, and how to do it, in a way that's easy and accessible.

PREACH LIFE CHANGE

When we are talking about discipleship, ultimately what we're talking about is changed lives. Always ask people to be thinking of how their life looks different after than before. How is their life changing?

In the Acts of the Apostles, the preaching of the apostles was all about announcing the Good News of the kingdom of God. That announcement led to incredible life change, and those changed lives formed the Church. That can happen at your parish, too.

SACRAMENTAL TOOLS

34

BAPTISMS ARE OPPORTUNITIES—TAKE THEM

It happened in those days that Jesus came from Nazareth of Galilee and was baptized in the Jordan by John. On coming up out of the water he saw the heavens being torn open and the Spirit, like a dove, descending upon him. And a voice came from the heavens, "You are my beloved Son; with you I am well pleased."

—MARK 1:9–11

Father Michael: Recently, I baptized my niece in a parish in my brother's community. The whole process was very frustrating. Even though the pastor didn't need to do much (since I was doing the Baptism), he made me, and my brother, feel bad about the whole process, sort of like we were an

unwanted intrusion. That was especially unfortu-
nate because my sister-in-law is new to the Catholic Church and, in her naïveté about churchworld,
actually thought churchpeople would be happy
about her baby and the Baptism.

Baptisms are turning points in parents' lives because they are part
of the transition from single life to married life, and maybe from
unchurched living back to church. Of course, the enormous change
children bring is part of the mix, too. Like all transitions, people have
a greater openness to God as they face the uncertainties of life. They
come to church because, even though they might not say it, on some
level they are looking for blessing and validation, not a hard time.

Tom: We've done it ourselves. In addition to making
baptismal prep a hassle, we made the mistake of
viewing this time as an occasion to catechize and
instruct parents about the sacraments. I used to
run our Baptism classes, and I put a lot of emphasis on the theology of the sacrament: the whole
history reaching back to the Book of Exodus, up
through Vatican II reforms, and eschatological con-
sequences—you know, just the sort of stuff new
moms love to sit around talking about.

It is all very beautiful and true and completely
irrelevant to parents who only want to show off
their baby, boast a bit, and plan the ceremony.
My Baptism class was a compelling lesson in how
much we didn't get it when it came to the lives of
our parishioners. And, of course, the parents were
obligated to attend, just to make matters worse.

On the other hand, I could see parents light up
when invited to discuss with other new parents the
joys and struggles, and the hopes and dreams, they
all hold for their babies.

The opportunity given to us at Baptisms, at its core, is not for instruction and catechesis; it's for celebration. Sure, we have a responsibility to share the treasury of Church teaching on this wonderful sacrament and ensure parents are properly prepared, but the greater opportunity is to build relationships that can lead to discipleship. If new parents come to us and they have a great experience, we win the right to be heard moving forward.

On the other hand, if we bludgeon them over the head with history and theology that they don't care about, and pistol-whip them with rules and procedures they didn't expect and don't understand, we'll have missed an opportunity. By all means honor and observe the laws of the Church, but don't use them as weapons.

Here are some practical things we do instead.

CHOOSE THE RIGHT INSTRUCTOR

Think about who on your team talks to families when they inquire about Baptism. Do you have a warm and welcoming person who is actually good at speaking to people who are perhaps new to the scene and don't know the right questions? Or does he or she make people feel as if they are imposing for wanting a Baptism? Look for the right person who can lovingly and enthusiastically walk with parents through the process.

REVISE YOUR FORMAT

Take a fresh look at your Baptism class. Whatever it looks like, and whatever else you do, stop calling it "class." Shape the environment into a more relaxed, relational experience. Give new parents the opportunity to share their story and show off their baby.

ESTABLISH A BAPTISM MINISTRY

Look at the celebration of Baptism itself. Do families feel as if this is a real celebration for their special day? Let it be all about them. Whether it's an individual or group baptism, extend the effort to make it personal, beautiful, and joyful. For priests, deacons, and parish administrators that might be challenging because you've already got a lot going on. That's why you want to develop a Baptism ministry, which consists of people who set up for the ceremony, greet guests, help with questions, and basically do everything except confer the Sacrament. There are mothers, and grandmothers (and likely some fathers and grandfathers), in your parish who would *love* to serve in this as their ministry.

It's become clear to us that as we've reshaped the whole process of Baptism in our parish into a more relational, engaging, and loving experience, it yields greater fruit in terms of young families who want to get involved.

In Jesus' own baptism, his Father spoke to him words of encouragement and love. Let's do the same.

35

WHEN IT COMES TO FIRST COMMUNION, PUT DOWN THE CARROT AND STICK

Whoever eats my flesh and drinks my blood has eternal life, and I will raise him on the last day. For my flesh is true food and my blood is true drink. Whoever eats my flesh and drinks my blood remains in me and I in him.

—John 6:54–56

Father Michael: I have a cousin with three children, each a year apart. Over the course of three years, I had conversations with my cousin and her husband about the experiences they had with their parish, specifically, the pacing of the children through the preparation for and reception of First Communion.

Every year, the process got more complicated and more and more frustrating for them. Over the years, the coordinator in charge of the program seemed to grow in her determination that it would be a fussy and labor-intensive project for everyone involved. Sister was especially vigilant that all the i's would be dotted and the t's crossed, and there were always more i's and t's.

For starters, she wanted to make sure each family was going to Mass on a weekly basis and "participating" in the parish (whatever that meant) before receiving first communion. Certainly, weekly Mass attendance is a great goal, but the way the coordinator went about it was the interesting thing. In the first year, she tried to ensure that families came to Mass by checking if their envelope was in the offertory. Of course, that meant Sister had to sit in the rectory basement on Sunday mornings alongside the money counters and sort through every single envelope by hand (and it's a big parish).

This requirement was widely ignored, but not for long. No envelope on Sunday ensured a telephone call from Sister on Monday. She had a strict three strikes you're out policy, and exceptions were rarely given (basically somebody better be dead).

By the second year, families figured out a strategy around this requirement. They created their own collection system. All the families in a given neighborhood or area would drop off their envelope at the home of the designated driver for the week; then the designee would go to church and place the envelopes in the collection. Sister had her spies, and when she discovered this trick, she prepared her counterattack.

By the third year, when my cousin's third child was preparing for First Communion, families were required to actually go to Mass as a family. How, you wonder, did she make them do that? After Mass (not before), each family had to personally sign in with Sister and personally hand her their giving envelope. A driver's license might be required. Sister was indefatigable, she was intrepid, and she won.

My cousins, meanwhile, have left the parish and stopped practicing their faith. After their third received First Communion, they never went back to the church.

Being cultural Catholics, they wanted their children to receive First Communion, and they were willing to jump through the hoops to make it happen. Were they playing games? Sure. Both sides were. And the game proved to my cousins that everything they ever thought was wrong with churchworld was true. The experience totally turned them off to churchworld once and for all. After the "value added" of receiving First Communion was no longer a factor, the Church held no value for them.

When it comes to First Communion, we find ourselves in the position of having something families want. Catholics who may only come to church on Christmas and Easter want their children to receive the sacrament (at least currently they still do). Certainly, their motives may not be what we want them to be. They come to us more because of the cultural overlay, but it is what it is, isn't it?

First Communion has become a celebration of children and a kind of graduation from early childhood, complete with all the usual clutter of cultural celebrations: costumes, cakes, parties, photos, and presents. This is regrettable perhaps, since First Communion is really about something much more important: an introduction to the fullness of the Eucharistic celebration. But it's not more important to them, at least not yet. They are coming to us, freely, willingly, and joyfully. That doesn't happen in churchworld much any more.

Why not take advantage of that enthusiasm instead of working against it? Surrender the need to manipulate and control, stop using the carrot of communion and the stick of church attendance and envelope use (or whatever your stick is). Direct your program, your efforts, your comments, and your celebration of the sacrament to the audience that might just come back and get involved in discipleship.

Christ instituted the Eucharist as a memorial of his Passion, so that we could remain in him and he in us. First Communion is a wonderful opportunity to introduce children into a growing relationship with Jesus Christ and, perhaps, to reintroduce their parents.

Don't approach the interest casually committed Catholics have in this occasion as the opportunity for behavior modification. Punishment and rewards will work if your goal is only to assure that no one takes advantage of you. They won't work if your goal is discipleship, though it is difficult and sometimes frustrating try to use this occasion as a discipleship-making event. Sometimes you will be taken advantage of. Sometimes, at least every once in a while, you will change hearts.

Ask yourself this one simple question: Would you rather be in the religious rule keeping business or the heart changing business?

36

MAKE CONFIRMATION INITIATION, NOT GRADUATION

It shall come to pass I will pour out my spirit upon all flesh. Your sons and daughters will prophesy, your old men will dream dreams; your young men will see visions. Even upon your male and female servants, in those days, I will pour out my spirit.

—Joel 3:1–2

You have probably heard this one before. A Presbyterian pastor, a Lutheran minister, and a Catholic priest serving in the same small town gathered together to share the joys and challenges of leading their churches. The conversation turned to a problem the Presbyterian was experiencing: "We have these pigeons in our steeple. They make a huge mess. They are noisy and loud and we can't get rid of them." The Lutheran acknowledged a similar problem. The Catholic priest chimed in: "We had the same trouble too, but we solved it." The other pastors asked how he did that. The priest responded, "We confirmed them. Never saw them again."

Probably everybody wants Confirmation to be a feeder system into high school youth ministry. Unfortunately, it often looks more like graduation than initiation. It effects the very opposite of what we want to accomplish. We know of very few vibrant and successful high school youth ministry programs in Catholic parishes (there are a few, just not many).

> **Tom:** Confirmation looks different in different dioceses. The Archdiocese of Philadelphia, my hometown, confirms in sixth grade. Other dioceses confirm later in middle school or high school, and in some places Confirmation of children happens at the same time as First Communion, as in the process of adult initiation. In our own Archdiocese of Baltimore, it is left up to the individual parish when to confirm. Many of the parishes with schools confirm in eighth grade, probably because the school parents demand it (thereby strengthening the graduation-confirmation association).

A lot of Confirmation programs emphasize catechesis, include a service component, and commonly require some kind of retreat experience. Unless the program is in a school (where they have to do it), leaders or youth ministers have the thankless task of coaxing and cajoling students through, and the dropout rate is high. In our experience, many young people just don't care.

Parents are behind the whole thing, and they cast themselves in the almost unwinnable position of getting their kids to go (to class, to Mass, and to the retreat) and then defending them when, inevitably, they don't or they "can't." In addition, parents' loyalties are often divided. While they are interested in their child receiving the sacrament, they're not very committed to their child preparing for it. Lacrosse tournaments and dance recitals are far more important (sometimes even more important than the actual celebration of the Confirmation liturgy).

It is not unusual for the parents to give up or, more and more, not even try. In our parish, at least three times the number of kids receive First Communion than receive Confirmation. Perhaps, in the future, there won't even be Confirmation "classes" of young people.

Tom: We struggled with Confirmation for years. The biggest mistake we made was trying to build our youth ministry program around it. When I first started out, there were about fifty or so students each year who would register for the Confirmation program in their freshman year of high school. I approached those fifty kids as my basic youth ministry group.

To hold on to this "core" group beyond Confirmation, I devised a cunning strategy that I was sure was foolproof. I moved the celebration of the sacrament from spring of freshman year to fall of sophomore year. Essentially, I was trying to buy time; the idea was to keep them in the youth ministry program into their sophomore year and then give them such an awesome experience that they would just have to come back, sacrament or no sacrament.

It didn't work. The week following Confirmation, right on schedule, the kids stopped coming. They got what they had come for, or rather, they'd gotten what their parents wanted. And here's a dirty little secret nobody wants to talk about: Unlike the sacrament itself, when it comes to high school youth ministry, not only do the teens not want it, but the parents don't either. Why bother? What's the point?

Discipleship? "No thanks, we got them through the sacraments; now we need a break."

Providentially, I moved out of youth ministry, and we found a youth minister with courage and creativity. Chris made the bold decision to put Confirmation on a different track. He built his youth ministry apart from Confirmation. In the beginning, that meant a much smaller program. Some weeks, only a handful of kids would show up, despite all his hard work and preparation. But Chris showed great faith and perseverance that eventually paid off.

Now our high school youth ministry program is growing, and it's healthy. Meanwhile, the Confirmation program has become much more meaningful. At one of our recent celebrations, our vicar bishop noted the vibrancy of the worship and the spiritual maturity of the students receiving the sacrament.

Here are the practical ways we've made our Confirmation program and our high school youth ministry more successful.

PROCESS

We decided that Confirmation preparation is not a *program*; it's a *process*. It's a process of spiritual discipline. High school students (not their parents) begin preparation anytime they choose, beginning in their sophomore year. But here's the deal: Confirmation isn't a feeder system for youth ministry; it's the other way around: youth ministry is the feeder for the Confirmation program.

MENTORS

Each candidate is assigned an adult mentor who regularly meets with the candidate, one-on-one, throughout the preparation process. This is a person trained for the ministry by the parish staff. The candidates can later choose a sponsor who stands with them as they receive the sacrament. Together with their mentors, the candidates write a vision statement establishing the spiritual habits that will form the foundation of the process.

ACCOUNTABILITY

Candidates themselves are responsible for remaining accountable for the habits, which is an acronym:

HABITS

Hang time with God: personal prayer and quiet time

Accountability with other followers of Christ: small groups

Bible: study and reflection

Involvement in the parish: mission or ministry service

Tithing or offerings

Sacraments: Eucharist, Penance, Eucharistic Adoration

The goal for these habits is for students to develop their own spiritual disciplines, so that moving forward into discipleship, they learn how to grow on their own.

The prophet Joel looks forward to the time in which we live, the time of the church. He sees ahead to the amazing gift of God's Spirit that we receive in the Sacrament of Confirmation. This gift, together with Baptism and the Eucharist, is a consecration into the Christian life that confers a mission. It is an opportunity for our young men and women to catch a glimpse of the amazing vision God has for their lives. Let's help them see it.

37

PEOPLE REALLY WILL COME TO CONFESSION—REALLY

Joshua said to Achan, "My son, give glory to the Lord, the God of Israel, and praise him by telling me what you have done, do not hide it from me."

—Joshua 7:19

The Sacrament of Reconciliation, Penance, or Confession has fallen into disuse over the last decades—deeply so, almost to the point of extinction. We know this is not because people have given up sin, so something else must be at work. Maybe they've given up a *sense* of sin, personal responsibility, and the need for grace. Do we just keep on doing what we're doing and pretend there is no problem, or cede the field and give up the fight? Can we restore this sacrament to the life of our parishes and the habits of our parishioners as a core value of discipleship?

Over recent years, we have experienced a dramatic increase in the number of our parishioners who will avail themselves of this sacrament at least once in a while. Here are the practical things we do to make it happen.

WE PREACH IT

At least once a year, we devote the entire weekend message to the importance of confession. We don't preach guilt and obligation; we preach mercy and grace. We preach healing—healing for our hearts and healing in our relationships; we preach conversion and life change.

WE MAKE IT ACCESSIBLE

The weekend after we preach it, we make it available and accessible. Among other times, we try to have confessors available during the whole weekend Mass cycle, recruiting retired priests to help us out. We also make the sacrament available all day on Good Friday, and extend its availability on the Saturday before Christmas, and on New Year's Eve—in other words, at times that are convenient when people might already be thinking about confession. We make it easy to go.

WE ENCOURAGE CHILDREN'S PARTICIPATION

We encourage parents to take their children, and when they do, they always make use of the sacrament themselves (their kids expect them to). This is a surprisingly easy sell for parents of younger children; these parents are awakening to the reality that they need an authority larger than themselves to help their kids grow in virtue. We also offer confession in our student programs, and they make use of it, too.

Joshua, the great man of God, finally and successfully led the people of Israel into the Promised Land. But even there, personal sin of the people was a problem, hurting the life of the whole community. Joshua understood the indispensible importance of confession, long before Jesus even instituted it as a sacrament and gave it to us as an amazing instrument of mercy and grace.

Your parishioners need this sacrament, and so does your parish. The wide use of it will powerfully contribute to growing healthy disciples.

38

USE ANOINTING STRATEGICALLY

He is not the God of the dead but of the living.

—Matthew 22:32

Prior to Vatican II, Anointing of the Sick was commonly called Extreme Unction. In practice, it had become the harbinger of death, and people stayed away from it as long as they could, really until all else failed. Ideally, Extreme Unction would be the last thing that happened to the dying, if their timing was right and they had the good sense to seize the opportunity of their anointing and go ahead and die. That way they could be assured full remission of sin and immediate entrance into heaven. As such, it sometimes became a game of chicken, and it was only possible because every neighborhood had their own local parish rectory filled with priests who, selflessly, stood on call 24/7.

Vatican II revived the Church's more complete understanding of this sacrament. It is not the sacrament of the dead. Like all sacraments, it is a life-giving encounter with the risen Christ for the living, who are in danger of dying and in need of healing.

Although the theology has changed, in many places the practice or at least the expectation has not. Priests are still being called at the last possible moment to anoint the dying. Clearly, this is a practice that is no longer sustainable. There are simply not enough priests to staff it. The guys who try to work under its weight experience a heavy burden that can wear them down and burn them out.

We can't do it, and we shouldn't even try. We have to learn to use the Sacrament of the Anointing of the Sick in the way that better serves the living. We have to use it strategically.

Over the last few years, we have become more strategic in our parish—more deliberate and premeditated—in administering the Anointing of the Sick. Here are some simple, practical steps to take.

STRATEGIC TIMING

Father Michael: I reserve a specific time during the week when I administer the sacrament. I have a staff member who keeps an ear out for opportunities to visit those especially or gravely ill. I cannot go and visit everyone in the parish who is sick every time, but that does not mean I cannot visit anyone. Andy Stanley calls this "symbolic leadership." Do for one what you wish you could do for all. So, about once a week, we identify someone (or several someones) in the parish whom I can visit and anoint (meanwhile, like many parishes, we have a wonderful team of generous parishioners who visit and extend pastoral care to all the sick on behalf of the entire community).

STRATEGIC ACCESSIBILITY

We encourage people to come to us for anointing when they come to Mass. Before they face surgery or after they receive bad news, they can request the sacrament while they are already at church.

STRATEGIC WEEKENDS

About once a year, we will offer Anointing of the Sick throughout a single weekend here at church. Of course, we explain the sacrament, what it's about, and whom it is properly for, and then we offer it immediately following Mass. It is a great opportunity to recognize as a community those among us who are seriously sick (many times we don't even know who they are) and raise up their suffering in prayer. Those weekends can be quite powerful for the whole congregation.

Anointing of the Sick is a spiritual comfort to the seriously ill, bringing renewed health and strength or victory in Christian death. Either way, it is a restoration of that which has become disordered. This restoration shouldn't be an afterthought or last resort. Rather, it should hold an honored place in our parishes that celebrates life in Christ. God is a God of the living.

39

BEWARE OF SELF-RIGHTEOUS SUPER CONSUMERS

One's enemies will be those of his household.

—Matthew 10:36

Father Michael: When I first came to Nativity, our daily Mass was offered at 9:00 a.m., and it had a large following. Given its time and the fact that it was daily Mass, it was not surprising that it almost exclusively attracted senior citizens. It was their Mass (although for many of them, Nativity wasn't their parish).

We assumed that these people were demonstrating spiritual maturity by their daily discipline. We were under the impression that they would be the most mature Christians in the congregation, with the fullest appreciation for the Eucharist, the deepest charity, the widest sense of service, and

158

that they would be the most generous givers. We also assumed this group would be our strongest supporters moving forward.

This was probably our biggest miss ever.

Don't get us wrong; there were some serious disciples attending our daily Mass and others who were well on their way (a lot further than we were, for sure). By no means, however, should we have made the assumption we did about this crowd as a whole. In the consumer exchange that our church had become, some of our daily Mass goers were the ultimate consumers, and their consumption established their righteousness; they were *self*-righteous. While the righteous are right before God in Christ and what he did, the self-righteous think they're right before God because of what they do.

The self-righteous are always and easily identifiable by their distinct lack of charity (a grumpy demeanor is often a telltale sign). We call them "self-righteous super consumers" (SRSCs).

It would be wrong to say our SRSCs contributed nothing to the life of the parish. They were, in fact, a reliable source of gossip and complaint. But mostly, they just consumed.

At one point, we built a new fellowship-style area in front of the church, which we called the café. It was intended to help develop a sense of community with our parishioners and serve as a place to welcome guests. Our SRSCs, who had quite vocally challenged and opposed this addition (and certainly did not help fund it), demanded use of this space following daily Mass. At first, we reluctantly agreed. Our reluctance was fueled by our concern that we were just making the problem we already had worse. Just for the record, we were. We created a clubhouse for the gossip and complaint club; SRSCs hung out there all morning. It was convenient, and of course, the price was right.

Eventually, we knew we had to do something about it: we had to kill it. We had to kill the culture we had created. It was brutal. What we did was move the daily Mass time to 5:30 p.m., when working people could also attend. What followed was a superstorm of bitter criticism to anyone who would listen, from the vicar bishop to the papal nuncio. We held our ground (just barely), and most of our SRSCs decamped to other parishes, thereby solving our problem for us. By the way, this mini-exodus had absolutely no effect on our weekend collections. What does that tell you?

Beware of SRSCs. It's not about daily Mass; it's about consumption in place of discipleship. Here are some practical approaches.

BEWARE

Expect SRSCs. They are indigenous to any religious setting, including yours. Recognize that you are not crazy when you find yourself challenged or troubled by people you thought would be your supporters and natural allies.

BE FIRM

Expect SRSCs to be dissatisfied. For years, we tried to placate this group and give them everything they wanted. And every time we did, they demanded more. Just set proper boundaries, maintain them carefully, and insist that your consumers observe them.

BE ARMED

Expect SRSCs to be armed and ready for battle. Understand that conflict will probably be inevitable with them, at least if you are changing or transitioning your church to a more deliberate discipleship-making enterprise. Your consumers won't like that at all, and they'll fight against it.

Jesus came to bring peace and reconciliation between God and human beings. To achieve that ironically but inevitably, involves conflict: between light and darkness, between good and evil, between righteousness and self-righteousness. He counseled his friends and followers to expect it, and not be so naïve as to think it will only come from external enemies.

Much as you might wish that your congregation is already a mature assembly of fully formed and devoted followers of Jesus Christ, just acknowledge they're not. Many of your biggest problems will come from the people already in your pews. Don't be confused, don't be surprised, and don't let it stop you.

40

SERIOUSLY, SEE WHAT HAPPENS WHEN YOU STOP ANNOUNCING MASS INTENTIONS

Therefore, since we have been justified by faith, we have peace with God through our Lord Jesus Christ.

—ROMANS 5:1

Anybody can request a priest to offer Mass for a specific or special intention: in thanksgiving, in special need, for the deceased, or many other such things. Usually this request is accompanied by a small stipend. It is a practice that has deep roots in the earliest history of the Church's liturgy.

Mostly, the only requests we ever received were Masses for the deceased, and they came in two ways. The first way was the daily foot traffic in the office requesting Mass cards. Typically someone is going to a viewing or visitation at a funeral home, and they bring the card as a kindness to the family.

We had a selection of cards, providing a range of choices from simply sentimental to badly baroque. The usual "offering" was five dollars, but we had a really fancy card for ten dollars if you wanted to go for baroque (sorry).

The card promised that Mass would be offered "for the repose of the soul" of the deceased. It's an idea relying on the Church's understanding that the graces that flow from the Sacrifice of the Mass can benefit even those who have already died. Wow, what a beautiful truth! But it's amazing how quickly beautiful things become less beautiful. You see, there was another kind of request we received. We'll call it "the insiders' special intention."

Like most parishes, we had something called the "Mass Book." It was simply a daybook for the year in which all the Masses were listed. Then, as requests for Mass intentions came in, they were recorded in the book. A big day around here was the arrival of next year's book. There were insiders who knew when that was; they waited for the day and lined up for it when it came. There was some kind of insider alert we weren't privy to that brought them out. They'd reserve all their special anniversaries for their deceased loved ones and—of course—all the marquee Masses, like Christmas, Easter, and Mother's Day, would fill up fast. Some people would buy fifty, even one-hundred dollars worth of Masses. These Masses became "their" Masses. A consequence of this commerce was the unspoken expectation that their intention got attention—from the altar.

Father Michael: When I first got here, I didn't know that. So I would start Mass as the Roman Missal asks us to—with the Sign of the Cross. But it had become the practice here to instead start Mass by announcing the intention: "This Mass is offered for (name the deceased), at the request of (name the owner), on the occasion of (name the anniversary or whatever).

Every time I forgot this, or got it wrong, I would get slammed after Mass. Very quickly, I learned my lesson, but I still got into trouble because visiting priests and weekend helpers would inevitably also mess this up, and that was always my fault.

There was one woman here who was a super consumer of Mass intentions. She had at least one every Sunday, sometimes more than one. She often had long, difficult to pronounce, hyphenated names in her intentions. If it was Sunday, that meant I was automatically messing up her Mass intention.

While canon law allows this practice, it also cautions, "Any appearance of trafficking or trade is to be entirely excluded" (Can. 947). Wow! We were way beyond *appearance*; our system was a clear-cut retail exchange.

We tried a few different tactics to improve this situation, discourage unhelpful expectations, and change the consumer culture that had developed around the practice. Admittedly, we stumbled and fumbled with this one for a long time, but here are three practical steps we eventually developed.

WE STOPPED ANNOUNCING INTENTIONS

Try that. This was greeted with complete indifference by the congregation at large and ferocious outrage by a small circle of consumers. If we had publically denied the Trinity or the Virgin Birth, they could not have been more offended. But it immediately and dramatically cut down on the number of intentions requested. Hmm. So what was the point of the practice?

WE STOPPED SELLING MASS CARDS

Actually, we discontinued the Mass cards as we had been offering them and started making our own. It's easy; anybody with a PC or Mac can do it for you. Here's the thing: Our new cards promise not Mass but prayer at Mass by the person giving the card. For most people it serves the same purpose because they have something to bring to the funeral home. And, in one way, it's more of a gift, because they are promising their own prayer.

We did have one woman who took a look at the new card and threw it back saying, "That's crazy; you expect *me* to pray for them? That's your job." But generally it has been well received. We also accept no money for the card. If they really want to make an offering we encourage them to make it in the offering at Mass.

WE STOPPED ACCEPTING INTENTIONS

All our Masses are offered weekly *pro populo* (for the people), and on a rotating basis for all the deceased, for those in need, for the sick, and so forth. We offer no more special intentions for individuals. When someone dies in our parish, we place their name in the Prayer of the Faithful, and we're happy to include other names that parishioners request. We also have a ministry that sends grieving families a card, with an additional pledge of prayer. Once a month, we offer a Mass specifically for the deceased of the past month as a way of honoring our dead and prayerfully standing with those who are grieving.

Mass intentions are a lovely custom with a profound spiritual value, both for the living and the deceased. When, however, they promote consumerism, when they communicate that church is an insiders' club for people who are buying their own salvation and getting their friends in on their ticket too, that's a problem. We are justified by faith in Jesus Christ, and that shouldn't be a mixed message in our parishes.

41

FUNERALS ARE SCUD MISSILES

The plans of the diligent end in profit, but those of the hasty end in loss.
—Proverbs 21:5

Scud is a name for tactical ballistic missiles developed by the Soviet Union during the Cold War and exported to many developing countries to cause global disruption—a goal they certainly achieved. During the Gulf War, these missiles were used widely by Iraq. The missiles could be launched from nearly anywhere and landed nightly in many varied and unexpected places. As this was the first war in history to be broadcast live, viewers would wait nightly, along with news crews, for when and where the next explosion would be and watch live all the ensuing chaos.

Funerals are like scud missiles. They are unexpected, and they immediately create, if not chaos, certainly disruption. It begins with a telephone call, any time, you know not when, and suddenly everybody stops doing what they were doing and gets involved. The schedule changes; your agenda is shot; and time is of the essence (because the funeral director, who, unlike you, is making money on this, wants to nail down all the arrangements as quickly as possible and get it in the newspaper). In other words, the funeral director's schedule becomes your responsibility; their urgency becomes your agenda.

Father Michael: The expectation I inherited was that as pastor I would do the funerals (*all* the funerals). Let's be clear what that meant; think about the extent of the expectation.

You've got to meet with the family (who probably aren't members and maybe aren't Catholics) to plan the liturgy: that means "selecting" the music and the readings (which is kind of funny because every funeral we've ever done has had virtually the same music and the same readings). This meeting is also about trying to talk them down from the ledge of whatever special features they've already planned on their own. ("Our niece plays the piano; we'd like her to do the music." "We invited Uncle Nick to read one of his poems; could we just do that instead of these readings?" "We want Dad's golf clubs on the altar.") This is also where you're very likely to get an earful of every gripe and complaint they have ever formed about the Catholic Church.

Then comes the "vigil" the evening before the funeral, when you lead a prayer service seemingly designed to make everybody really confused because nobody knows what's going on. They don't know when, or if, they should sit or stand; they have no idea what they're supposed to say.

On the next day comes the funeral Mass, where you will probably see very few of your own parishioners, but maybe lots of unchurched family members of the deceased. That sounds like an opportunity for evangelization. It's not. These people do not want to be in your church; it starts out simply awkward, and at communion it becomes uncomfortable.

When it comes to the homily, nobody really wants one; everyone expects a eulogy in which the deceased, regardless of the real record of his or her life, is at least beatified, if not outright canonized. If you have the additional burden of not even knowing the deceased, this can be tricky.

The funeral also includes the committal service, but before you get there you've got to do something truly odd and sometimes dangerous. Everybody gets into their cars and forms a "procession" to the cemetery. It goes really slowly and sometimes creates major disruption on the streets and highways of your community. Plus, other drivers don't necessarily know this disruption is a funeral (or they don't care), so they can get annoyed and angry. After the committal, there is sometimes an invitation to lunch, where you can spend more time with people you don't know (and will never see again), who are uncomfortable around you because they haven't been to church since last Christmas.

Meanwhile, everything you planned on doing is still back at the office waiting to be done.

Respectfully, we would love to see our bishops' conference address this issue, because it is a hugely intrusive one. While there has been widespread discussion about reducing the number of weekend Masses and Holy Days of Obligation to make things more manageable for clergy and parish staffs, funerals are much more work. Changing or modifying expectations at a national level would be an incredibly important step forward for our parishes. The *Order of Christian Funerals* already provides a Funeral Liturgy Outside of Mass in which deacons and properly trained ministers can preside. If this service became more the norm than the exception, it could transform the lives and schedules of parish priests and staffs everywhere. It would also be a more comfortable setting for unchurched guests and a more appropriate context for the music and eulogies that many families are requesting. Of course, the Mass is the principal celebration of the Christian funeral, and for those well churched, it should be the norm. But could parishes not offer a monthly or seasonal Mass for all the recently deceased, and week-to-week and day-by-day, celebrate funerals outside of Mass?

This is beyond our purview, of course, but we have tried to make things a little less dysfunctional. We've developed some policies and structures to manage better current expectations and make sure that an incoming funeral doesn't disrupt everyone and everything. Here are some suggestions we offer in making sure funerals don't entirely disrupt the other work we need to do.

RECRUIT VOLUNTEERS

Get some volunteers who can help with funerals. The best place to look for help is going to be with retired people. Give the funeral director their cell phone numbers; let him call them first, not you.

Train your volunteers to meet with the family. Sure Father, you can step in to say hello, greet the family, and pray with them, but you don't have to spend an hour of your time to figure out that, Oh yeah, that song we want is called "On Eagles Wings."

Volunteer ministers can also be on hand to help set up on the day of the funeral, greet guests, generally make things easier for the celebrant [and all those guests], and decide where the funeral flowers are placed.

ESTABLISH CLEAR BOUNDARIES

If you are a priest, put boundaries around your schedule, especially if you are the pastor. Often families will ask for the pastor simply because they know who he is or because they look upon him as a way to upgrade their funeral. However, they are often more concerned about having the funeral at the day and time that works for them. That is their number one priority. If they can get the pastor, all the better.

> **Father Michael:** Increasingly, the requests I receive for funerals come with a day and time already decided, regardless of my availability. That's fine. I do not do funerals on Mondays; if I am scheduled to be off or away, I do not do funerals at all. If you want me to do it, we have to find a mutually workable time. You can't choose the time and then just expect me to fit you in. I have been widely criticized for these positions; I hold on to them anyway.

BEWARE OF CONSUMERS

Be especially aware of consumers. Some people are just shopping around for a church, and there is really no opportunity for ministry. If they're not your parishioners and they're just looking for a place and time that's convenient, don't feel guilty about just saying no.

At the same time, stay attuned to the special funerals. Sometimes there are funerals that come in that just demand undivided attention on our part. After September 11, we held a funeral here for a young man who died in the World Trade Center. That was an extreme example, but other examples of special situations easily come to mind: the death of a child or student, death as a result of a tragedy or accident, and the passing of a key volunteer.

We mean no disrespect to grieving families; losing a loved one is the hardest thing of all, and the Church should make every effort to be present and pastorally sensitive in those situations, commending the dead to God, strengthening the hope of the living. But this doesn't mean you can't manage the situation in a way that works better for you, your staff, and your real mission, and it doesn't mean you have to cede your mission to manage this ongoing need.

Don't be terrorized by funerals. Plan diligently to handle this challenge well.

KIDS AND
STUDENTS TOOLS

42

DO SOMETHING FOR MY KIDS, YOU DO SOMETHING FOR ME

"Why were you looking for me?" he asked. "Did you not know I must be in my Father's house?"

—LUKE 2:49

Tom: Once you have kids, your life changes. You have a burden that never goes away. It is constantly there. You struggle with adjusting to the complexities of children and their needs. You can no longer just think about yourself or pick up and go wherever you want. Almost every decision you make about time and money, and everything else, is made with your children in mind.

At every turn, you constantly question yourself whether you're doing right by them. When things do not go well or they have a bad experience, it is

one of the worst feelings a parent can have. When
things go well, it is a tremendous win.

This was an incredibly important lesson we had to learn when it came
to our approach to church. If children and students enjoy coming to
church, not only do their parents enjoy church more, but also they
benefit from a much-needed service as well. A former colleague of ours,
Carol, said it this way: "Do something for my kid, you do something
for me."

This is true for families with children at any age level. When children are in kindergarten and even younger, we have an opportunity to
make the church accessible and relevant. Many couples first go back
to church, after years of being away, because they want to give their
kids a solid foundation, and they instinctively know they need support
from a higher moral authority than themselves.

It's very easy to make the most of this with young families. Just
providing a nursery program for babies and little children gives couples
a break and a breather from relentless parenting, and it makes your
church experience worthwhile for them, even if you don't have much
else to offer. Couples get to actually sit together for an hour, maybe
hold hands, and listen to a message that might very well add value
to their lives. Eventually, they'll come to know and appreciate the
Eucharistic celebration in a way that they had not before (and might
not ever if they're chasing the kids around during Mass). If kids are
in safe, clean, fun environments, complete with great volunteers who
love them, they will be excited to come back and bring their parents.

As children move into grade school years and beyond, providing
great experiences, programmatically and relationally, takes a little more
effort, but need not be labor intensive or expensive. Children's ministry
and student ministry aren't "add-ons" or extras to the life of our parish;
they are at the heart of it. Here are three practical things you can do
to make these happen where you are.

NURSERY

Find a space where you can host a Sunday nursery, ideally a space adjacent to your church. Clean it, childproof it, and supply it with appropriate (safe, cleanable, nonplush) toys (you probably won't have much trouble getting these donated). Give it a fun name, maybe even a theme; decorate it, and make it look like a place a kid from your neighborhood would want to be. Build a team of volunteers who can each staff it a couple of times a month for an hour or so (making sure they have the necessary background checks and child protection training before they begin). Be consistent with providing this service no matter how often you are able to offer it. Consistency is key so parents can come to depend on it.

LITURGY OF THE WORD FOR CHILDREN

If you don't currently offer a Liturgy of the Word for children, consider adding it to at least at one of your weekend Masses. If you have one, take a fresh look at it, or consider expanding it to other weekend service times. Look at where it happens in your building, and think about improving that environment, if possible (it is possible). Consider ways in which you could make it more vibrant, dynamic, and interactive.

MIDDLE SCHOOL

Don't forget middle school students. Where in your weekend is there something for them? How are they being included in the life of the community? Short of anything else, provide them with service opportunities associated with the weekend Masses: in fact, they can help out in the children's Liturgy of the Word.

The Lord Jesus was introduced to the Temple as a baby; later, as a child, he came to feel at home there, recognizing it was his father's house. Our parishes should feel the same, and when they are, we are better serving both our children and their parents.

43

AFTER SECOND GRADE, SCHOOL ISN'T COOL

Let the children come to me; do not prevent them, for the kingdom of God belongs to such as these.

—MARK 10:14

Tom: Not so long ago in our part of the country, if you were a practicing Catholic, you sent your children to Catholic school. This was certainly the case when I was younger. I went to Catholic school, just like all the Catholic kids in my neighborhood. There was barely a religious education program to speak of in my parish.

That program was called CCD (Confraternity of Christian Doctrine), and it consisted of maybe a couple dozen kids who were more or less second-class citizens in our parish. In the '80s, that began to change. My mother took over the program in our parish as the first paid staff person in the history of our parish. She started part time. As a kid, I can remember her preparing for a meeting with the pastor to make an argument that she should become a full-time staff member as the program, and her workload, grew. She showed him how many hours she was working and how she really needed to be full time to do her job correctly and completely. It was an uphill battle, but she made her case and became full time (way to go, Mom!). Now, there are more kids in her religious education program than in the parish school.

My home parish is an example of how the world has changed over the last few decades. The vast majority of Catholic children do not attend Catholic schools. Meanwhile, the backup plan for their religious instruction and formation has become CCD, which in many places has been repackaged as "religious education" or PSR (parish school of religion).

To put it mildly, this has not been an unqualified success. Essentially, we took what was happening in a full-time school curriculum and tried to jam it into a one-hour, once-a-week program and offered it over thirty-five or forty weeks of a program year. At Nativity, it never worked, given the time constraints and the incredible commitment the model demanded of teacher-catechists that pretty much ensured the program would always be under staffed.

But that's not the only issue. Here at our parish, we went out of our way to make the whole experience look and feel like school: desks, blackboards, textbooks, and even a bell. Here's the problem with that: after about second grade, most kids don't really like school. In our parish, first and second grade were always twice as big as third grade and probably ten times as big as eighth grade.

Knowing that kids don't like school and certainly don't want to spend their evening or weekend free time in another school environment, we have tried to make our religious education program look and feel different. Here are three practical things we did to transform our program into a positive environment for kids.

FUN

We decided our program was going to promote fun. Kids like fun, and they want to be a part of environments where they know they'll have it. We can win influence with them when we are helping them to enjoy themselves. We've been criticized on this point, so we want to be clear:

- Is there instruction in the doctrine of the Church? Absolutely.
- Are we forming children in faith? Certainly.
- Are children being introduced to the sacraments? Positively.

But none of those values is incompatible with an environment and experience that neither looks nor feels like school. Our program promotes fun; fun promotes learning; learning promotes growth; and growth promotes discipleship.

STRUCTURE

To establish this plan we began by changing the structure of the program. We set aside the classroom approach for a small-group model and made the transition progressively over the course of several years. Our small-group model is built around relationships, led by leaders, not teachers, who do not really teach so much as invest in children relationally. Their main goal is leading the children into a growing relationship with Jesus Christ and with one another. The relationship with Christ and fellowship with one another takes on such value that children willingly become lifelong learners in their faith.

Each small-group session includes an engaging Bible story presentation and relevant message (usually connected with the weekend's gospel reading), discussion, and worship. Parents are given resources to go deeper at home during the week. Children continue with the same small group and catechists from year to year, deepening their relationships with one another.

ENVIRONMENT

We also changed the environment of our programs. The actual small-group environment does not look like a classroom. We got rid of blackboards, bulletin boards, and textbooks; we don't have desks. Instead, kids sit on the floor on carpet circles. Our spaces are still somewhat austere, because they were built as classrooms, but one day we hope to transform them into truly irresistible environments.

A poorly planned program of religious education is more than a lost opportunity; it's a sin—one that we were guilty of for many years. Our program was placing an obstacle in the way of our children's approach to Christ, who told us not to do that. Christ is attractive to everyone, including children. Let's make sure his Church is, too.

44

TREAT STUDENTS LIKE ADULTS

"Ah, Lord God!" I said, "I do not know how to speak. I am too young!" But the Lord answered me, "Do not say, I am too young." To whomever I send you, you shall go; whatever I command you, you shall speak.

—Jeremiah 1:6–7

We both had a professor at Loyola University Maryland who has had a great influence over our lives. Sue introduced us to each other and continues to support us. While she had a (well-deserved) reputation at the college as a tough professor, most people who actually took her classes respected and liked her.

In retrospect, it's easy to see why she engendered such respect and indeed loyalty from young people: she treated us as adults. In so many settings, students (think teens) are treated without respect and in a condescending manner. Sometimes, in some places (like churches), they are held suspect or mistrusted. At Nativity, there were so few young people that when one actually showed up, they elicited stares and their clothes probably elicited disapproving comments.

As a church, we can be different. And if we are, we will be a more attractive place for teens. When it comes to student ministry, treat them as adults, extend respect and trust to them, honor them and their unique personalities, and recognize and promote their gifts and talents. Here are the practical things we do to try to make sure that happens in our middle school and high school programs.

ACT AS IF STUDENTS DESIRE GOD

We treat students as adults by acting as if they really desire to know God—even if they don't—and are interested in spiritual growth— even if they're not. If we take the necessary steps to effectively show them how our faith is relevant to their lives, they find their way to our programs, sometimes bring their friends along, and usually stay involved.

Our student programs don't include a lot of games (though fun is important in creating a relaxed and casual environment). They do include worship, led by student musicians, and a serious and challenging message given by our director of student ministry, Chris, or another member of his team. This message often follows the same theme of the weekend homily that students have heard at Mass.

ENCOURAGE SMALL GROUPS

We treat students as adults by challenging them to get into a small group (just as we challenge adults). There, we strive to cultivate authentic conversations, where students can really share what is going on in their hearts and lives. They don't have to pretend they are better than they are, or try to be something they are not. They know they will not be judged or censured, just challenged to grow.

URGE STUDENTS TO USE THEIR GIFTS

We treat students as adults by giving them an opportunity to use their gifts and abilities in our parish ministries and mission outreaches. Just as we don't want adults to simply be consumers, we don't want high school students to be growing up that way either. Students are hard-wired to serve, and it can make the weekend experience of church far more effective and engaging when they do.

When called, the prophet Jeremiah thought he was too young to get involved and serve. God thought differently.

Treat teenagers with respect. Give them access to service and talk to them about growing spiritually and maturing in their faith just as you would adults. Treat students as you would adults, expect good things from them, and you will be astounded by the results.

MONEY TOOLS

45

FUNDRAISERS CREATE SIDEWAYS ENERGY

Be rich in good works, to be generous, and ready to share, thus accumulating as treasure a good foundation for the future, so as to win the life that is true life.
—1 Timothy 6:18–19

Bob is a friend of ours whose daughter began attending a Catholic school a few years ago; he told us this story. Throughout her first year, he felt constantly assaulted and eventually inundated by the school's fundraisers: candy bars, wrapping paper, and pizza kits. There was an annual black-tie dance with both silent and live auctions, a fall bull roast, a spring crab feast, a 5k run, and a harbor cruise. When the next school year rolled around, he walked into the principal's office, checkbook in hand, and said, "Okay, Sister, no more wrapping paper and candy bars; just tell me, how much? How much do you want to educate my daughter this year?"

Father Michael: Sometimes fundraisers can become too much. Recently a priest friend shared with me how exhausted he is, how burned out he feels, and how he was even considering taking a leave of absence or just walking away from the priesthood entirely. What was the problem? He inherited all these fundraisers, which he now needs just to pay the bills.

In our day, we've had our share of fundraisers. Most of them were undertaken to fund stuff we wanted that the budget couldn't support. We never liked doing them; they never felt good; and in our experience, they never felt very good to our parishioners either. But we just assumed they were a necessary, indispensible part of parish life. We need money to do ministry, so we need fundraisers.

If you're a Catholic school, we'll concede, you probably do need fundraisers. We don't know anything about running a school, so we don't know if that's true, but we'll just concede the point and stick to what we do know.

What we will not concede is that, more often than not, fundraisers are not the way to fund a parish. They wind up diverting staff efforts from actual ministry; they can quickly burn out volunteers; and they distract parishioners from the message of the Gospel. These problems alone serve as reasons enough to get rid of them. There is an even greater problem with fundraisers, however, which is far worse.

Fundraisers always create sideways energy that casts parishioners in the role of consumers and puts the focus on raising cash rather than growing disciples. Put another way, you gain momentum, you gain ground for the kingdom, when someone decides to give to the church, but all you gain is cash when you do a fundraiser. You don't move your people forward.

Do the difficult thing; do the seemingly impossible thing: get rid of fundraisers. Here are the practical ways to get started.

KILL JUST ONE FUNDRAISER

And don't start with the one that is considered a "community event," a revered tradition that is an expression of heritage or culture. Don't start with one that everyone loves (or says they do). Go with the one people will be glad to get rid of, the great, big, ugly, labor-intensive one that you have to manufacture energy to make happen. Kill that one. Then the next year, kill another one.

ADJUST YOUR BUDGET

At the same time, make the adjustments you need to make in your spending and your budget. This might mean some belt tightening (cutting things) at first. That's okay; this exercise is a discipline and, like all disciplines, will take time to root.

When you can, restore those items to your operating budget if they are truly integral to your mission. Fund them by your offertory collection.

PERSIST

Ignore the naysayers who say it can't be done, and don't let the prophets of doom scare you. Do it, but do it in prayer. Pray and fast about this transition. Preach about it, too. Help the parish to understand that the operations of the parish will be funded by the worship offering, or they won't be funded and probably shouldn't be anyway if no one wants to pay for them.

It is our responsibility to raise up givers, not funds, because it's our responsibility to make disciples, not money. As you honor God, trust that God will provide the money, because he will. Here is the beautiful truth: When we go where God is blessing and we focus our energies on making disciples, the funds we need for ministry will follow. The money won't come as quickly as fundraisers; you will have to wait, but it will come later and in greater supply. Forget fundraisers. Be rich in good works.

46

PASS THE BASKET AS SELDOM AS POSSIBLE

Let your "Yes," mean "Yes," and your "No" mean "No."

—Matthew 5:37

Father Michael: When I first came to Nativity, I had no experience as the pastor of a parish, so I would ask pastor friends of mine for advice. Early on, one very successful pastor of a huge parish told me, "Michael, you have to pass the basket as often as possible. Every time you pass the basket, you'll make money." He explained that each week he took up two collections. The first was the usual collection for the operations of the church. Once a month, of course, the second collection was the one requested by the diocese or bishops' conference. But subsequent weeks would see additional collections labeled for various needs: monthly maintenance, seasonal campus cleanups, the winter fuel fund, snow removal, and Christmas decorating.

I took his advice and discovered that he was absolutely right. Every time I passed the basket I made money.

Wait. So then, why is this chapter called "pass the basket as *seldom* as possible"?

Let's face it: while second collections raise more money, they don't raise much more. When the basket comes by a second time, most people ignore it; some only throw in pocket change—their leftovers. Think about it: why is your second collection a fraction of your first; why is there far more loose change than substantive giving? Because most times when people give to a second collection, they don't even know what they are supporting, or they've learned not to care.

Over time, we came to realize that if we passed the basket twice we would get more money, but what we didn't get was more mature givers. When people give because we trick them into it, or guilt them into it, or cry about the busted boiler, they're giving at a kind of entry level. That's Giving 101. When people give because they recognize that ministry costs money and it's their responsibility to give, that's Giving 201. When people give because they want to honor God, that's graduate-level giving.

For us, passing the basket once is a symbol of our straightforward, disciplined, and transparent approach to giving. As disciples, our parishioners need to be giving. We invite them to do it in the Eucharist—as an offering, a worship offering. We want our parishioners giving in their place of worship as an act of worship.

Let your "yes" be "yes" and your "no" be "no," as scripture counsels. Make your parish giving be all about giving and not manipulation. Discipline your parish to pass the basket as seldom as possible. Eventually, not initially or even quickly, but eventually you will be leading people to become more mature givers. And that is a great gift to them.

47

SEAL UP
THE POOR BOXES

Is this not, rather, the fast that I choose: releasing those bound unjustly, untying the thongs of the yoke; Setting free the oppressed, breaking off every yoke? Is it not sharing your bread with the hungry, bringing the afflicted and the homeless into your house; Clothing the naked when you see them, and not turning your back on your own flesh?

—Isaiah 58:6–7

Of all our assertions about money, this one could seem the most radical, the least sensitive, and even a bit heartless; and you might leave this chapter disagreeing with us. We didn't even agree on this one for a long time. This chapter's axiom can't be right, can it?

Besides, sealing up the poor boxes may sound as if we don't want to give to people outside our church and that we only want people giving to us, but that is not our heart here.

The Bible clearly and consistently instructs, and the Church every-where teaches, that we must care for the poor, especially through our giving. This kind of giving has been associated with the celebration of the Eucharist from the earliest days of the Church. It is a time-honored tradition everywhere. We're not questioning any of that. Our concern with poor boxes is that, like fundraisers, they don't really build mature givers and neither do they really create concern for "the poor."

Like second collections, our poor boxes typically yielded pocket change at our church. Every once in a while we would discover a fifty or hundred-dollar bill, which we assumed was either an act of guilt relief, or just someone who wanted to give but didn't want to give to us.

When it comes to giving and churchworld, we try to keep it very simple. Our aim is that people give in the weekly offertory collection. We believe that keeping giving as simple as that, without any confusing options, helps develop more mature givers.

As for the poor, we give as a parish out of our collection. Each week we set aside a percentage of our offering for our missions in Haiti and Nigeria, as well as our missional partners here in Baltimore. Admittedly, it is a small percentage, but it is vastly more than we ever made in the poor boxes. The funds for Haiti support a school lunch program. In Nigeria we have funded various projects, including wells to provide fresh water for several communities. Our local efforts are likewise designated in ways that parishioners can see and support.

Whenever we preach on money and generosity, we encourage parishioners to calculate their giving to the parish together with their charitable giving beyond the parish as part of their tithe. We challenge them to get involved in supporting good work and kingdom-building efforts wherever they're found.

The poor are not a monolith. There is a whole wide world full of issues and concerns that lead to poverty and its attendant problems. While as disciples we cannot be actively aware of all of these issues, God certainly calls us to learn about some of them. We are to take interest, on a deeper level, about issues of injustice such as pro-life advocacy, human trafficking, homelessness, fatherlessness, and illiteracy. When people give to poor boxes, they are safeguarded from confronting any of these issues head on. As we give, we should grow in our understanding of what our gifts support.

In everything we do, we want to be driving people toward discipleship. Ultimately, we want our charitable giving and mission outreach to do that, too. The prophet Isaiah reminds us that it is God himself who is calling us to develop a much deeper relationship with the poor. Freely fasting from our affluence, we are to join ranks with them in the mutual work of the restoration of creation.

48

LOSERS GO FOR FRUIT

I planted, Apollos watered, but God caused
the growth. Therefore, neither the one who
plants nor the one who waters is anything
but only God, who causes the growth.... For
we are God's coworkers.

—1 Corinthians 3:6–7, 9

From time to time, we are solicited by consultants who are trying to sell us their services, promising increased giving. There are lots of them out there, and they have various approaches.

One organization arranges a direct mail campaign in which parishioners receive what looks like a personal letter from the pastor (though it's really a computer-generated letter from the company). The letter names the specific dollar amount the donor gave to the parish in the previous year and challenges them to give a higher amount, also cited in the letter, in the coming year. If the parishioner doesn't respond to this appeal, another letter is generated, and then another. The company promises that their straightforward letters get results, though most would agree it is aggressive and annoying.

Another group has an in-pew approach. Everybody gets a pledge card in the middle of Mass, and then you essentially lock the doors and stare everybody down until you guilt them into filling it out. Plenty of people do.

There are other approaches, too. What the ones we've seen have in common is that they're going for short-term increases.

These efforts are like plucking fruit off of a tree without any consideration for the health of the tree. You can approach giving in your parish like that, and you'll be successful in raising additional money in the short term. But we think, as author and psychologist Henry Cloud says, ultimately "losers go for fruit."

Making people feel guilty or uncomfortable and surprising them or even embarrassing them into giving is one approach to raising money. You can go for easy fruit, but a more winning strategy is to plant fruit-producing trees and cultivate and grow them into more mature givers.

Over the last few years, we've seen significant increases in giving in our parish, and the level of giving continues to grow. We have seen these increases without the assistance of a single consultant.

Here are the simple, practical steps you can take.

TITHING

Get to know what God's Word has to say about giving and tithing. Start tithing yourself, and challenge your parish staff and major volunteers to do the same.

PREACHING

Remain steadfast and determined, be clear and consistent, don't be distracted by the naysayers or discouraged by the critics. Keep preaching giving and tithing.

PRAYING AND FASTING

Pray and fast for your givers and your potential givers. Raise them up before God in thanksgiving for what they have given and in hope for what they will give.

Like St. Paul teaches us, don't just go for the fruit: plant and cultivate fruit-bearing trees. Take a long-term view. You can't rush it. It takes time to grow great givers. But God, who causes the growth, will grow them in your congregation.

49

KNOW HOW TO ASK FOR MONEY

The people rejoiced over the free-will offerings, for they had been contributed to the LORD wholeheartedly.

—1 CHRONICLES 29:9

It takes money to do ministry. We need money to pay staff, turn on the heat, and of course, fund programs and services. Ministry requires money, but you've got to ask for it to get it, and you've got to know *how* to ask, if you're going to be successful, at least successful over the long haul.

After one of our annual Stewardship Sundays, a comment was made: "These guys know how to ask for money." We considered that a great compliment (and hopefully it's true). Here are some things we believe we currently get right (after years of getting it wrong). We think you can do them, too.

WE GIVE

Before we ask anyone for anything, we give first—and so do our staff members and volunteer ministry leaders.

WE TALK ABOUT MONEY ONCE A YEAR

While we talk about money as often as it comes up in the lectionary, because it was one of Jesus' favorite subjects, we talk about giving to the parish only once a year. Let's say that again: We talk about giving to this parish only once a year. That means, when we do it, we have to do it well.

On that weekend, we ask each individual or family to fill out a commitment card. The card isn't really to provide us with reliable information on what to expect in giving levels (it actually doesn't). So why do we do it? The card is about commitment. We want members of our parish to make a plan for their giving. The card is both a tool to help them plan and, once complete, their written plan. We especially encourage them to plan to give electronically through what we call our automatic worship offering.

In our message on stewardship, we also encourage members to be percentage givers. We personally accept and honor the biblical giving standard of the tithe, or 10 percent, but this is a difficult message to hear for many people (people as in Catholics). So, while we teach the tithe, we challenge them to start somewhere by picking a percentage of their income to give. We want parishioners to be percentage givers on the path to larger percentages.

WE HARDWIRE GIVING TO VISION AND MISSION

We work hard to help parishioners understand that their giving is funding what God is doing among us. So, on Stewardship Sunday, we're going to be reexamining our mission statement and painting a convincing and compelling picture of our vision of God's vision for our parish.

In 1 Chronicles 29, David raises money to build the Temple. He does it well. He makes his offering first, he asks leaders to join in, and then he makes an awesome argument. David says that the gifts of the people would build the house of God and raise up their nation above all the nations on earth. 1 Chronicles records that "the people rejoiced." When is the last time that happened in your parish?

Ask for money well, and people will give freely to the Lord and find joy in doing so.

50

SHAPE THE PATH

Then the Lord said to Moses: Why are you crying out to me? Tell the Israelites to set out.
And you, lift up your staff and stretch out
your hand over the sea, and split it in two,
that the Israelites may pass through the sea
on dry land.

—Exodus 14:15–16

Not too long ago, we attended a church conference all about stewardship and giving. One of the speakers stood up and proposed the following scenario. Suppose, he said, his daughter had a rare disease. There
was a cure; however, treatment would be costly. There was no time to
lose; effective treatment required urgency. The financial assistance of
everyone present was needed, and a collection was taken. An appeal
like that would be compelling, and doubtless many hearts would be
moved to help. But probably few would. Why?

To demonstrate his point the speaker asked, "How many of you
have two hundred dollars or more in your wallet right now? Don't be
shy; this a Christian group." In a room full of hundreds of people,

only a handful raised their hands. Then he asked, "Okay, how about one hundred dollars?" Only two or three more hands were raised. It was only when he got to twenty dollars that there were very many hands. Finally, he asked, "How many of you have checkbooks on you?" Almost no hands at all could be seen. We live in a society that less and less carries cash and more and more exchanges money electronically. The way people spend is also the way they will give.

It is difficult for most people to become generous givers; really, this is very difficult. If we do not establish and promote opportunities for people to give in ways that work better for them, they simply won't be giving to us, even if they want to.

We use an axiom we learned from Dan and Chip Heath in their book *Switch*: you've got to "shape the path." When it comes to giving, we've got to shape a path that takes potential givers where we want them to go.

Move beyond cash, and create opportunities and systems for people to give electronically. Here are a few practical ways you can do it.

GIVING ELECTRONICALLY

Set up an electronic funds transfer (EFT) account at your bank and then begin encouraging your regular givers and envelope users to switch their giving to it.

Only a couple of years ago, we had very few families giving in this manner, and we didn't think anything about it. Mitch, our operations director at the time, challenged us to recognize the impact this kind of giving could make. We took a fresh look at the situation, reconsidered, and changed our whole approach; we started promoting EFT.

Every year on Stewardship Sunday, we vigorously encourage members to join the program. When people step into membership by joining our parish and come to our new members program, we take that opportunity to invite them to give in this way as well. At this point, probably half of our regular givers give electronically. That's a start.

We've branded the program "Automatic Worship Offering." We still provide giving envelopes for those who wish to physically make an offering in the Mass itself (or are sheepish about appearing to not be making an offering).

GIVING ON THE WEB

Make online giving available on your website. Set up a donation button on your home page where people can't miss it and can give online using their credit or debit card. Make sure your donate button is easy to find and easy to use.

GIVING ON THE GO

Consider a giving "kiosk" in your lobby. They can be expensive, but a "giving kiosk" is an incredibly convenient way to give; people just swipe their cards on their way in or out of Mass, while they're thinking about it. The kiosks quietly remind people to give.

Even easier than that, start thinking about mobile giving, which is giving on the go. At this point, most people probably own a smart phone and live their life with it. They should be able to give with it, too.

In fact, you need to be on the lookout for the next steps in your giving strategy, because technology will continue to change the way we give.

Moses was directed by God to establish a path for the people where no path existed. To move forward, they needed a plan and a path. That's what we need for our givers. Passing the basket is a great symbol of worship giving, but when it comes to giving itself, we need new paths.

51

BE RESPONSIBLE/
BE TRANSPARENT

After a long time the master of those servants
came back and settled accounts with them.
The one who had received five talents came
forward bringing the additional five. He said,
"Master, you gave me five talents. See, I have
made five more." His master said to him, "Well
done my good and faithful servant. Since you
were faithful in small matters, I will give you
great responsibilities."

—Matthew 25:19–21

The Bible is clear as can be: everything belongs to God. We are stewards of what he has put into our hands. To raise up disciples of Jesus Christ who are mature givers, we must clearly and creatively communicate this message and live it out in our own lives, especially when it comes to how the parish spends money. All the money we have has been given to us. Givers place their trust in us that we will profitably use it to advance the work and the movement of God's kingdom. When you stop and think about it, that's an intimidating responsibility that demands transparency.

Here are the practical steps you can take.

COUNSEL

Every pastor is required by canon law to establish a financial council or committee, but having one and actually using it can be two very different things. Turn to people who know something about finances and accounting or just people who are smart and get them on board. Meet regularly; keep minutes of your meetings.

Share all necessary and pertinent information with members; insist that honest and open discussion is not just permitted but also encouraged. While ultimate decisions belong to the pastor or pastoral life director (or sometimes the bishop), they need to listen to this group and take their counsel seriously. If their recommendations are not taken, there should be a clear explanation given.

MISSION AND VISION

Drive one overriding question through your budgeting process and financial planning discussions. Does the money we are spending support and serve the mission and vision of the parish? We are sometimes surprised when, at least in hindsight, the honest answer to that question is "No, not really." That's why we've got to keep asking ourselves the question, over and over again. Make sure your staff is asking that question, too.

Even when you can answer that question in the affirmative, you then need to consider the cost-benefit analysis: Is this expense the most effective use of our funds? Is it having the greatest impact toward mission and vision?

PRAYER

Pray about the parish's money and your stewardship of it. Pray and fast that you will be a responsible steward of God's money. Ask the Holy Spirit to search your heart from time to time and show you ways you can be a more responsible steward.

The Bible celebrates God's ownership of everything: his ownership, our stewardship. This responsibility calls forth our very best efforts, though it shouldn't paralyze us into inaction. It should spur us to greater efforts, to be more faithful and more fruitful, because the master gives more to those who are.

STAFF TOOLS

52

WIDEN THE GENE POOL

The next day John was there again with two of his disciples, and as he watched Jesus walk by, he said, "Behold, the Lamb of God." The two disciples heard what he said and followed Jesus. Jesus turned and saw them following him and said to them, "What are you looking for?" They said to him, "Rabbi" (which translated means Teacher), "where are you staying?" He said to them, "Come, and you will see."

—John 1:35–39a

Tom: In college, I had a history teacher who had a saying she would often repeat while lecturing on the royal dynasties that once ruled Europe with absolute authority, and now no longer exist. She would describe how the royals, especially by the late nineteenth and early twentieth century, were all related to one another (just look at their portraits; they all looked alike). Then she would wave

her arms in the air and lament, "Widen the gene
pool! Widen the gene pool!" Her point was that so
many of the problems leading up to the calamity
of World War I were the result of the isolation, insu-
lation, and inbreeding of Europe's leaders.

History tends to repeat itself, and we've seen this in our parish. When
it comes to ministry, there is a tendency to go back to the same people time and time again. New projects or ministries come up, and we
turn to the usual suspects—the people whom we *always* ask—to get
the job done. Regardless of where you are on your journey as a parish,
this will be a temptation, if not a deeply entrenched practice. We have
people whom we are comfortable talking to or asking for help because
we know they will say yes.

Asking someone new to volunteer time to a ministry or project
takes more work, and its outcome is always a little uncertain. When we
ask someone new, we risk rejection, and we don't like rejection (maybe
it brings back memories of those awkward middle school mixers?).
Sometimes we are just too tired or too busy to think of someone new
to help with a project.

Inbreeding will create problems. When we get in that mindset, we
eventually burn out the good volunteer ministers we have. Either they
keep helping out of guilt (which is never a good reason for serving), or
they continue to serve but with increasing anger in their heart (which
is never a good attitude when serving).

We had one volunteer who served us in many ways for a few years.
Unfortunately, we overused her (and "used" is the appropriate word).
For her part, she liked to be the go-to girl and made herself available
and, eventually, indispensible. Meanwhile, she developed a vast sense of
entitlement, as if we owed her (which we sort of did). At some point,
she stopped taking direction; at another point, she started giving it.
She became a problem, and eventually we had to fire her. She left the

parish with great bitterness and in her wake there were gaping holes that had to be filled.

Since then, we have learned that we need to constantly invite new volunteer ministers into our work. We need to widen the gene pool. We love to team up newcomers with veterans and keep widening that pool. The people you invite into your ministry today can be your trusted stalwarts tomorrow.

Jesus began with two, who became twelve, who became seventy-two, who became three thousand, who . . . well you get the idea. Healthy ministry should always be all about widening the gene pool.

53

GET THE RIGHT PEOPLE ON THE BUS

Pharaoh said to Joseph: "Since God has made all this known to you, there is no one as discerning and wise as you are. You shall be in charge of my household."

—Genesis 41:39

In his book *Good to Great*, Jim Collins shares the best practices of successful business organizations. The book is well worth your investment and a must-read for any church leader. In his research, Collins used strict, data-driven criteria for comparison of the performance of different companies trying to do the same thing. He identified a number of features that inevitably distinguish the truly great companies from the merely good ones. Collins observed that the great companies got their start on greatness by getting the right people "on the bus" (i.e., in the organization). Only after they got them on board did they deal with getting them in the right seats—their place in the organizations.

Often we get this backward. We ask *what* before we ask *who*. *What* should we do to solve our problems or reorganize our parish? *What* should be our strategy going forward? Those are important questions, but Collins argues they are secondary to *who*, as in *who* should be on our team. He discovered that great companies ask who and then what.

When trying to lift a new ministry off the ground, turn a church around, or start over again (or whatever we're trying to do), we often run to the details. But the answer to the question—the real way forward—is not a plan. Plans are needed, but if you have the wrong person or people leading whatever it is you're trying to do, it will never succeed. The solution is not a plan; it's a person.

As a parish, we were famous for simply grabbing whoever was available and filling holes, hoping for the best. Sometimes we were lazy, sometimes we were desperate, sometimes we were just not careful, and sometimes the wrong person just wanted it and we let them have it. Meanwhile, if we've got too many of the wrong people around, the right people will never get on the bus.

Here are the practical steps we take to try to make this a priority.

GET THE WRONG PEOPLE OFF THE BUS

This is so difficult to do. We are not going to sugarcoat it—you already know it anyway and you know you've got to do it. Release people when you know they are the wrong fit or they're just not working out (or they're just not working period). Do it as gracefully as you can, but get them off the bus. By the way, this absolutely includes volunteers.

BE WILLING TO WAIT

We have learned the value of patience; we're willing to wait. This can be so uncomfortable when we feel an urgency to fill a position or get moving in a new direction, but rushing to fill a position, staff or volunteer, is hardly ever going to get you the right person and can lead to a lot of wasted time and money, and probably emotion.

Be willing to wait and invest in the people already working for you (for free). The solution to whatever you're trying to solve or staff is probably not "out there"; they're most likely in your parish. Your next best hire is your current best volunteer, and your next best volunteer is in your pews. Get to know the talent you have at hand.

KNOW WHO YOU'RE LOOKING FOR

We ask "who can do this" or "whom do we hire" based on three important, indispensable criteria we picked up from Bill Hybels, pastor at Willow Creek Church in South Barrington, Illinois: character, competency, and chemistry (*Courageous Leadership*, 80).

Character means that we hire or place in a key volunteer position people who have integrity and good hearts.

Competency also matters. Every job requires certain abilities. Of course, some knowledge and skills can be learned on the job, if a person is willing to learn. However, a person must have some level of competency and skills to get on the bus.

Chemistry simply means you get along with them and they can get along with you and the other members of a team. You like one another, and they will work well in your staff culture.

The story of Joseph in Genesis is a wonderful story of achievement and success, despite daunting difficulties. Joseph's secret was simply using the gifts and talents God gave him in the places God sent him to serve.

Personnel issues will always be a part of parish life. People take energy and effort. They can disappoint you and hurt you; they're worth the effort anyway. But do yourself a favor: Get the right people on the bus and the wrong people off, and you will go further faster as an organization.

54

TALENT ATTRACTS TALENT

And in his love for David, Jonathan renewed his oath to him, because he loved him as he loved himself.

—1 Samuel 20:17

We knew a pastor who had a terrible choir; they were just awful, although he always talked about it as if it were great. On special occasions or holiday liturgies, inevitably after communion, when they finally finished their screeching, this guy would stand in the pulpit and adamantly announce to the congregation, "That was wonderful!" Then he would proceed to lead the applause, and he kept clapping until everyone joined him. He was bullying the congregation into saying bad was good.

Celebrating and rewarding mediocrity is demoralizing to parishioners, and it sends a clear message to the unchurched that there is nothing here of value. Talent is, in fact, so rarely associated with churchworld that when people come across it in church, they're surprised or even shocked. They think it is some kind of anomaly, or that it just doesn't belong. We have a member of our staff who is an excellent speaker. After one especially fine presentation, a parishioner made the comment, "Wow, why doesn't she stop wasting her talent and get into television." He didn't understand the insult he leveled at us and missed out entirely on the fact that having an impact on people for eternity is a pretty good use of anybody's talent.

What we are doing in our parishes is more important than anything else that is happening on the planet. Doesn't that deserve the best? Talent, and the excellence that follows from it, honors God and most successfully serves our mission. That's why pastors and parish leaders must be on the lookout for talent, and using it, when it is uncovered.

Is the woman who is serving as cantor at the Saturday evening Mass the most talented person available to lead the singing, or just the person who wants to do it? Be on the lookout for musical talent in your pews. Is the chair of your financial council the pastor's golfing buddy or someone truly gifted with money and finances? Look for the smart people around you who can advise you and get them in positions of influence.

Is your children's minister or DRE someone with a heart for kids or just the next person in line for the job? Is she on the lookout for other people with that talent?

Watch for talent and use it when you find it and here's why: Talent attracts talent. As you promote the talent you have, more will be attracted to your team.

The Bible tells the beautiful story of the friendship shared by David and Jonathan. They had so much in common: they were strong, they were resourceful, they were smart, and they were fearless. In short, they were pretty talented guys, and they became best friends, because talent attracts talent. Talent always attracts talent. Use it. Promote it. Reward it. Celebrate it.

55

WORK WEEKENDS

It is lawful to do good on the Sabbath.
—Matthew 12:12

Tom: When I came to work in church, I never really gave a great deal of thought to what my schedule would be. For a number of years, I conducted myself pretty much as if I had a nine-to-five, Monday through Friday kind of job. And, as long as I did, I struggled to get the work-life balance right—a huge problem for many people working in churchworld.

Father Michael: Strangely enough, I could say the same thing. Coming to work in a parish, I did not shift my thinking about working weekends. Instead, I would try to arrange my various weekend work activities around my weekend leisure activities and social engagements, sometimes to the detriment of the quality of my work.

Our family and friends expected us to work this way, and we wanted to anyway. It was only when

> we both, finally, accepted the glaring reality that we
> work weekends that our weekends began to feel
> better. No kidding, this is a very emotional thing,
> and we see it played out in our staff, too. When
> someone comes to work here, you can tell if they've
> made the conversion or not, and if they resist long
> enough, they will eventually leave. It creates too
> much tension and strain to be on a parish staff and
> pretend your weekends are your own.

To be a happy and productive parish staff member, you have to acknowledge that you work weekends, or at least some significant portion of it. Your prime time, when you see your people and (not to be coarse) where you make your money comes on Saturday and Sunday.

Help your staff members change their minds about weekend work and approach it as the high point of their whole week, not just an afterthought, or one more thing to do. Schedule the rest of the week from the perspective that it's all about the weekend. On Mondays, acknowledge and celebrate the weekend that was. On Wednesdays or Thursdays, have a check-in meeting and update everyone about how the weekend preparations are coming. Take Fridays off, as your Sabbath time for rest and renewal on the eve of your big days.

For our churches to be successful, we've got to change our minds about the weekend. Jesus challenged the Pharisees to think differently about the Sabbath. Of course, they refused. And, well, how many Pharisees do you see around anymore?

56

BE LEADERS WHO LEARN

King Darius wrote to the nations and peoples of every language, wherever they dwell on the earth: "May your peace abound! I decree that throughout my royal domain the God of Daniel is to be reverenced and feared: For he is the living God."

—Daniel 6:26–27

When a new staff person joins our team, it is always enjoyable to watch them discover, often to their surprise, how difficult it is to work in a parish. We have especially relished the several occasions when someone has come to us from the business world or another professional arena, thinking they know everything about running a church and assuming it's going to be easy. Church is not easy.

Parish work is challenging and one of the most daunting challenges is the varied aspects of the work. There are many different constituencies, and so much to learn when it comes to laboring in the trenches of a local church. We confront personnel issues—hiring and developing staff as well as recruiting, training, maintaining, and motivating volunteer ministers. There are operational issues: budgeting, maintenance, technology, and record retention. There are legal and canonical issues, as well as security issues. We are in the communication business, so there are communication issues such as clarifying and communicating vision and better understanding the culture we are trying to reach. We are dealing with the public, so public relations, consumer complaints, and pastoral care are concerns. This list doesn't even touch on the sacraments, the weekend experience, children's and youth ministry, or religious education—and on and on.

Now, layer on top of everything we just listed the little fact that we live in a world of accelerated change—where everything is in rapid movement and constantly changing. To lead people successfully into a growing relationship with Jesus Christ, we need to be leaders who learn and keep learning as a matter of daily discipline.

Rick Warren says, "The moment you stop learning, you stop leading." When we stop learning, we lose the moral authority to lead others. As we learn, we grow. As we continue to learn and grow, we gain moral authority to lead people to new places. Learning keeps us fresh, young, and sharp. Learning also keeps us humble and protects us from pride. When you learn, you must humbly acknowledge that you are incomplete. Learning opens us up to the grace God wants to share with us through others.

Here are the practical steps we try to rely on when it comes to learning and growing.

READ

Read books, blogs, and articles. There is more information available out there than ever before. Get your hands on everything you can. Listen to podcasts, DVDs, and audio CDs in the car, or when you're working around the house. Be discerning certainly, but be open to the many places that can provide information you can use in ministry. Some of our favorite authors and books are listed on the *Rebuilt* website. Don't be reluctant to turn to Protestant and evangelical resources when it comes to evangelization, small groups, giving/tithing, and other things. They do better than most of us.

REFLECT

This begins by reflecting on experiences. What happens to us in the course of our ministry can be an excellent teacher if we'll stop to consider it (and pray about it). After you have an event or finish a season, or anything major happens in your church's life, take time to reflect on it personally and as a staff. Honestly evaluate what you've done. Look at what worked and also what didn't. Look at mistakes and missteps, and when it comes to staff departures, subject them to scrutiny.

REPLICATE

Visit other churches, including Protestant and evangelical ones. Go and see what others are doing; get to know what their weekend services are like. You can do much of your visiting online. Consider attending a conference that so many growing churches around the country offer throughout the year, usually at very affordable costs. Filter what you see through the lens of your Catholic faith, but remain open to what it is you can use and imitate.

In the Book of Daniel we read the story of a king who did something that kings do not often do: he admitted he was wrong, and he changed his mind. The young man Daniel taught him a lesson, and to his credit, the king was smart enough to go ahead and let himself learn. Be like that as you lead your parish.

CRITICAL TOOLS

57

PREPARE FOR BATTLE

Be strong and steadfast! Do not fear nor be dismayed, for the LORD, your God, is with you wherever you go.

—JOSHUA 1:9

If you do anything in your church, there will be comment, criticism, and complaint. Maybe we better say that again: if you do *anything*, there will be comment, criticism, and complaint.

When you begin to make changes in your church, you will face conflict, perhaps serious conflict. Some of the conflict comes because, by nature, people in churchworld are more conservative and therefore more resistant to change. People come to associate human traditions with the will of God and then hold on to them for dear life and fight for them to the death. Most of it is emotionally driven, which means it can get mean and ugly, fast.

In transitioning a church to a more evangelical approach, conflict is inevitable, but there are some ways you can prepare for it and make it less disruptive. Below are a few lessons we learned from our experience.

PRAYER

Here is a suggestion (and it's not really a suggestion; it's an indispensible necessity): if you are planning any kind of transition, or new initiatives, begin with prayer. You are going to need to hear from God, and you are going to have to be talking to him, so start there.

COMMUNICATION

Inform the appropriate people in your diocese, as well as colleagues at neighboring parishes, of what you're doing. They're going to hear about it anyway, and if they hear from you first then they will have a better understanding of what is really going on and maybe they will watch your back for you. We speak from experience on this one, because we really dropped the ball here and sometimes left our bishop in the dark. That was a mistake for which we owe him an apology, but it didn't really set us up to move further faster either.

DAMAGE CONTROL

Do what you can to keep the turmoil contained. Parishes have been damaged and even destroyed when parish leaders amplified a personal conflict into a parish-wide one.

In the Bible, Joshua was charged to lead the Israelites from the desert into the Promised Land. When we are trying to make changes in our churches so that we focus on evangelization and discipleship, that's what we are trying to do. Moving people from a barren place to a fruitful one, and there will always be resistance and conflict in the process.

Joshua was a great leader and a mighty man of God. He fought many such battles, and through them all remained clear about something we tend to lose sight of. Underneath all the other battles is the real battle, the spiritual battle we are in as believers. We are fighting the power and principalities of this world that do not want us to take ground for the kingdom. Prepare for *that* battle and stay strong.

58

CARDS ARE GOOD; LETTERS ARE BAD

With all vigilance guard your heart, for in it are the sources of life.

—Proverbs 4:23

When it became clear to us we were starting on a new path and headed in a very different direction in the life and mission of our parish, we expected some pushback—we got it.

- We got it when we changed anything. It came from unhappy consumers who did not like change.
- We got it when we tried new things. It came from cynics and naysayers.
- We got it when we started challenging people to grow, serve, and give. It came from people who didn't want to do any of those things.

- We got it when we started learning from Protestant churches. It came from closed-minded Catholics who felt it was their duty to defend the deposit of the faith.
- We got it through the whole process of church transition that we made from passive participation to active evangelization. It came from passive parishioners who just didn't want to be active participants.

The pushback came in many forms, most notably letters. When your mail arrives and there are cards, you can relax. People send cards to be nice and say thanks or other kind things. Cards are good. Letters are bad. If someone goes to all the trouble of writing a letter, it's not going to be good news.

The letters we received followed a typical template. The writers always started by stating how long they had been in the parish (as their essential qualification for complaining). Inevitably, they continued by asserting that everyone else feels just the same way, only they are courageous enough (or selfless enough or whatever) to step forward. Next comes the complaint itself, followed by a string of other complaints, all strung together as if some secret plot to destroy the parish was now being revealed.

If you try anything in this book, you will get a letter about it, and it won't be nice. You are not going to please everybody, and some people are going to push back and write letters. Don't be surprised or upset when you receive those letters. Don't let them paralyze you into inaction or make you rethink your vision, and don't allow the people who write these letters to set your agenda. Criticism is part of the price of leadership.

Jesus was criticized all the time by the Pharisees and other religious leaders. He was criticized for healing on the Sabbath. He was criticized for eating with sinners and tax collectors. His hometown became so critical of his message they tried to kill him. He even took criticism from members of his own family.

When you receive a critical letter, consider the source and tone. Letters that are simply angry and intentionally hurtful should not be given much consideration. Anonymous letters should not be read. Having said that, you can still learn from your critics. Most of those letters will have some nugget of truth that can help you grow. Learn from that truth and move on.

Proverbs provides wisdom we need when it urges us to guard our hearts. When you are in ministry, this is especially important.

If you don't want to be criticized, get out of ministry; go do something that nobody cares about and that makes no difference to anyone. If you stay, accept the fact that criticism is inevitable. Jesus promised us that if we are with him, we will be opposed and persecuted. If we are making inroads for the kingdom of God, the evil one is going to come at us. We can expect that, when we are gaining ground for God, we will be opposed. Often it doesn't mean you are doing something wrong, but that you are doing something right. Criticism may actually be confirmation that you are doing God's will.

Never let praise go to your head, and never let criticism go to your heart.

59

DON'T BE UPSET WHEN THE WRONG PEOPLE LEAVE

I am the true vine, and my Father is the vine grower. He takes away every branch in me that does not bear fruit, and everyone that does he prunes so that it bears more fruit.

—John 15:1–2

Father Michael: I remember the day very well. I opened up the mail to find a giving envelope ripped into tiny little pieces, accompanied by a letter from a parishioner, a very prominent parishioner, announcing, with great drama, that she was leaving the parish. As a new pastor, who had never experienced this before, the episode upset me to my core. As I was stewing in self-pity and doubt, a friend came by. He was older and wiser and laughed it off as something to be expected. He then offered to take me to lunch. It was only much later that I

237

learned what a blessing that turned out to be. That
woman had been creating drama and intrigue in
the parish for years, long before I ever arrived. Her
departure was a gift.

If you start doing the right things, the wrong people will leave your
church and that, respectfully, is a good thing.

- By wrong people, we mean people who reject the vision you have
  and will never go where you are going.
- By wrong people, we mean problem people, people who have issues
  that they're not dealing with and that they don't want to deal with.
  You name the problem, and guess what? *You* become the problem.
- By wrong people, we mean angry people who bring their anger to
  your church.
- By wrong people, we mean hurt people who, in their hurt, hurt
  people.
- By wrong people, we mean dramatic people who are always spin-
  ning stories and stirring up drama.
- By wrong people, we mean people who are simply consumers who
  get insulted when you challenge them to grow as disciples.

We're not suggesting any of these people are bad or evil; they're just
people who are not happy in your church (or with you) and probably
never will be.

A couple of years ago, we had a problem with a key volunteer. The
staff member to whom he reported became concerned that this volunteer was serving for some unhealthy reasons, and those motivations
were beginning to play out in his ministry. So the staff member shared
her concern about the minister's emotional health and asked him to
take a break from his service. Instead, the volunteer and his family
decided to leave the parish. To his credit, he left fairly quietly, but it
still upset our staff member. It shouldn't have.

As staff, we have come to say to one another, "you earn your wings," when someone leaves the parish because of a tough, but necessary, call one of us has had to make. Again, we don't mean to sound disrespectful, but it happens to everyone who works in churchworld, and it's always kind of interesting for us to see the beginner's shock when it happens to them for the first time.

If you become intentional about evangelization and remain consistent, the wrong people will begin to leave.

Don't take their insults and drama personally. Don't feel as if God is somehow disappointed with you because they have left. If people leave because you are challenging them to grow and be concerned about outsiders, that shows you are leading in the right direction. When the wrong people stick around, the right people suffer. When the wrong people leave, it actually makes your parish healthier.

Jesus compares the body of believers to a fruit-bearing tree. To be fruitful, regular, seasonal pruning will be necessary. This is not only to be expected, it is necessary for healthy growth. Don't be upset when the wrong people leave. It's okay. We can all still be friends in heaven; we just need to be in different parishes until we get there.

60

DON'T BE SURPRISED WHEN THE RIGHT PEOPLE LEAVE

So sharp was their disagreement that they separated. Barnabas took Mark and sailed to Cyprus. But Paul chose Silas. . . . He traveled through Syria and Cilicia bringing strength to the churches.

—Acts 15:39–41

Father Michael: We had a member of the church who was very supportive of our early ventures. When we started making changes and moving in a new direction, he became a fan and a financial supporter (at a time when we desperately needed it). We considered him a friend and loved his whole family. They were bright, cheerful, positive, and encouraging. We all smiled when we saw them coming.

Eventually, they left the parish.

> **Tom:** I had a great volunteer who gave hours and hours of her time to the church. She organized service trips and all kinds of youth programs. She was a reliable advisor, and she and her family were close friends of mine.
> Eventually, they left the parish.

Sometimes the "right people" leave your church. They are people who have given their time, energy, and financial resources. If you stay in parish work long enough, you won't only see the wrong people leave but also see the right people leave, people you love who have worked with you in the trenches. These departures are wrenching and heartbreaking, and from time to time they will happen. Why? There are several reasons.

We've had the right people leave our church simply because their friends and family didn't like us. They left because they got tired of being on the receiving end of criticism. They chose their friends and family over us.

We've had the right people leave our church as we've become clearer and more consistent about our vision and strategy. In the process, these people come to realize that while there was something here they liked, they just weren't buying into the whole picture we had begun painting.

We've had people leave our parish who faithfully stayed by our side through a leg of our journey but were done traveling. They were willing to go only so far, but then no further.

We've had the right people leave our parish because we made some decision they just could not agree with. They left out of a sense of principle. For example, at a certain point in the evolution of our strategy, we took a strong stance on tithing and offerings (we started preaching what the Bible teaches). Some people, who were good people, took strong exception to it, and they left.

We've had the right people leave because of miscommunication or missteps we've made.

We've had the right people leave because we took them for granted. We just assumed we would have their support and didn't invest enough relationally; we weren't as grateful to them as we should have been.

We've had the right people leave because we stuck them with some ministry job that they never really wanted and kept them there. They left to get out of the job.

When the right people leave, it usually forces us to do some soul searching. Many of the reasons we've named are beyond our control; some are just beyond our ability to manage; we cannot do anything about them. Other times, it has clearly been our fault. But we are human, and that is going to happen.

In the Acts of the Apostles, we read the surprising story of a fierce disagreement between Paul and some of his associates in ministry. Eventually they separated. But the Bible also tells us they continued in ministry and continued to be effective, strengthening churches.
The right people will leave your church. Do not let their leaving define you as a bad friend or a failure. Grieve the loss, and use it as an opportunity to learn and grow. Figure out why they left. If there are changes you can make in your leadership to prevent the same thing from happening again, make those changes. Thank God for the time you did have those people on your team.

And leave the door open for them to come back. They might.

61

SAY YOU'RE WRONG WHEN YOU'RE WRONG; SAY YOU'RE SORRY (EVEN WHEN YOU'RE NOT)

When the news reached the king of Nineveh, he rose from his throne, laid aside his robe, covered himself with sackcloth, and sat in ashes.

—Jonah **3:6**

As parish leaders, we will make mistakes. We will get many things wrong, and, let's face it; there is something deep down in human nature that does not like to admit when we're wrong. It's been that way from the beginning. When God asked Adam in Genesis 3 why he sinned, Adam said, "The woman you put here with me—she gave me fruit from the tree, so I ate it." When God asked Eve why she sinned, she said, "The serpent deceived me."

When we refuse to take responsibility for what we've done wrong, we abdicate our position of leadership, just as Adam and Eve gave up their leadership role in paradise. While our pride keeps us from admitting our own sin and mistakes, ironically, we respect people who can acknowledge theirs. We especially admire leaders who can stand up and admit they were wrong. It shows strength of character, and it further strengthens character.

Admitting mistakes will actually strengthen rather than lessen your position with staff and parishioners, and if you're moving, if you're changing, and if you're growing, you'll probably have a lot to apologize for.

- Sometimes your decisions or actions will hurt people unintentionally.
- Sometimes people will feel overlooked or left out.
- Sometimes they will be offended that you failed to provide them with what they thought they needed, or deserved.

Besides what you actually get wrong, you might have to apologize for what you get right. As a leader, you may have done nothing wrong, but somebody's feelings were hurt as a result of what happened in the organization. The higher you move up in the organization, the more opportunity you'll have to apologize. If it happens on your watch, good or bad, you own it. If need be, you must take the hit.

Say you're sorry, even when it's not your fault. Say you're sorry, even when you're not. We do not mean that you should be insincere. What we mean is that you cannot wait for your feelings or even for the facts to guide you when making an apology. Don't let the lack of an apology get in the way of your mission and your vision.

Jonah, and probably everybody else, was shocked when the great king of mighty Nineveh was willing to repent and say he was sorry. Who knows how he really felt, but that's what he did, and he lost no time in doing it. In saying he was sorry, he saved the city. Be like that; say you're sorry.

Make the first move and say you are sorry about anything and everything. You will be moving your parish further faster when you do.

You can skip the sackcloth and ashes bit though. You don't want to overdo it.

62

ADMIT YOU DON'T KNOW WHAT YOU'RE DOING

Trust in the LORD with all your heart, on your own intelligence do not rely; In all your ways be mindful of him, and he will make straight your paths.

—PROVERBS 3:5–6

Over the course of many years, we struggled with Christmas, specifically Christmas Eve. We knew it was an incredible opportunity to reach people disconnected from Christ and his Church, but our building simply couldn't handle the crowds we experienced within essentially a three-hour window on that one evening. We tried various strategies, but nothing seemed to work or solve the problem, and all of them left us feeling frustrated.

Tom: One day, Michael found himself stopped at a light in front of the Maryland State Fairgrounds, a sprawling facility that just happens to be up the street from us (you can read the whole story in *Rebuilt*). He thought, "How about doing Christmas Eve here?" It seemed like a crazy idea, but the more we thought about it, the more it seemed like a great opportunity. We enlisted two key volunteers and got them on board. As we planned for that event, we began to realize that moving our whole church operation to another location for a single evening was a big job, and one entirely new to us. We found ourselves starting our planning meetings with this prayer: "Lord, we don't know what we're doing, but you do; guide us."

That prayer was essential to us as we set out on a new path. In fact, it was the most important prayer we ever prayed in the process. It helped us to come humbly before God and pray a very honest prayer. It helped us in other ways, too. Admitting we didn't know what we were doing actually took some of the emotional burden of the project off our shoulders. Praying that prayer made us realize it was okay that we didn't know what we were doing. It helped us to be more confident in our heavenly Father who is in control of everything.

If we are to be the kingdom-building movement God wants us to be, we will be constantly entering new territory. We will be launching new programs, undertaking building campaigns, test driving creative ways to enlist volunteers ministers, and on and on. Building God's kingdom requires us to go where we have not been before and do what we do, not know how to do it.

In other words, the exercise we are engaged in is inherently risky and scary. When we are in new places doing new things, it can be intimidating, even overwhelming. The temptation will be to play it cool or pretend we have it together, which only makes it more stressful. The next time you face a new opportunity or project and begin forming a team to make it happen, pray this prayer: "Lord, we don't know what we are doing, but you do. Guide us." You will notice your faith and confidence in God go up and your stress level go down.

The Bible urges us to live our lives, and certainly lead our parishes, with a radical sense of dependence on God—radical, as in *with all our hearts*. If that's how he wants us to be, why would we ever do otherwise?

63

GET OVER IT

Father, forgive them; they know not what
they do.

—LUKE 23:34

Feeling offended, holding on to hurts, and nursing grudges are all
a part of human nature. We so often fall into the trap of endlessly
replaying someone's thoughtless remarks or careless, insensitive actions.

Everyone is vulnerable here, but if you're a leader, you are especially
so, and if you're leading anything in churchworld, you've pretty much
got a target on your back when it comes to hurts and offenses.

- If you run a children's program, hypersensitive, overprotective parents will be assaulting you with their demands and their complaints,
  and you're going to want to take it personally.
- If you're a youth minister, you'll inevitably take criticism from
  unhappy adult leaders and diffident, difficult teens, and you're going
  to want to take it personally.
- If you're the pastor, you'll get it from every direction, and we know
  you too are going to want to take it personally.

The opportunities in ministry to be offended or hurt are myriad. Any change in anything will bring conflict, and sometimes it *is* quite personal. Staff members and volunteers can misunderstand our motives or misrepresent our views. Parishioners can be unkind, and employees can be unfair, even disloyal.

Expect it. Anticipate it. Then get over it.

Feeling offended is only natural, and you probably have plenty to be offended about. Get over it instead, because feeling offended only slows you down and distracts you from the more effective ministry you want to be about. It is an unnecessary, though powerful, emotional drain that can seriously hurt your heart.

But, it could be even more serious. Ours is a spiritual work, and when we encounter difficulties and setbacks, they are spiritual difficulties and spiritual setbacks. When we find ourselves in conflict, it is always and ultimately a spiritual battle. Here are our tips.

TALK TO GOD

Get over it by bringing your offense to God in prayer. Journal about it, talk to God about it, spend time before the Blessed Sacrament, and hand it over to him there. Every offense that hurts our heart is an opportunity for God to heal and strengthen us. Our Father is a healer and wants to heal your heart and soul so that careless words no longer wound you.

TALK TO SOMEONE

Get over it by speaking to someone else about it, too. Find a trusted friend (maybe somebody from your small group, your confessor, mentor, or spiritual director) who is willing to hear you out and let it die there.

TALK TO THE OFFENDER

Get over it by forgiving the offending person, from your heart. Talk to him or her, if you can. If you can't, have an imaginary conversation with that person if it helps. Share how you were hurt, and offer forgiveness.

Among the lifesaving and life-changing lessons our Savior gave us was his final one, from the Cross. There, he forgives the people who are in the process of killing him. Think about that: not just people who have hurt him in the past, but also people who are currently about the business of doing it. That's the example he's left us.

Whatever you're getting offended about probably doesn't exactly measure up to what he had to be offended about, right? So get over it. As you learn to bring your wounds to God, ask him to heal your heart and forgive the people who offend you, you will be offended by less and less. Offenses will roll off of you, and you'll have more energy and time to make disciples of Jesus Christ. Most often, those who have hurt you really do not know what they're doing, so don't spend any time there. Get over it, over and over again.

FUN TOOLS

64

CELEBRATE WINS

There will be more joy in heaven over one
sinner who repents.

—Luke 15:7

Ever notice that Sundays come every seven days and that weekends
come every six? There is always more ministry to do. There is always
the next homily to write; there is always another funeral to be planned.
We don't ever leave the office feeling, "Okay, everything is done. I'll
have to think up some more work to do." Working in a church can be
a grind. There is always more we can do.

Because of these things—more new people to reach and more lost
people to find—it is vital that we stop from time to time and celebrate
"wins."

We define a win as any positive movement someone makes toward
a growing relationship with Christ and his Church.

- When an unchurched or dechurched person comes to our parish
  for the first time and has a great experience—that is a win.

- When someone enrolls in our automatic worship-giving program—that is a win.
- When someone responds to a message and gets into a small group or begins serving in ministry—that is a win.
- When someone starts reading the Bible or carving out a daily quiet time for prayer, or when someone returns to Confession for the first time in a long time or finds time for daily Mass or Eucharistic Adoration—that's a win.

Any move toward Christ is a win, and if we don't stop and celebrate, then we can easily become burned out as staff members and volunteers. On the other hand, celebrating wins serves as motivation to keep going and fuels our efforts moving forward. Here are the practical things we do to make sure it happens.

DEFINE WINS

Celebrate wins by defining them. What's a win in your setting? If you are on a team or have a staff, sit down and do that together. Make sure you're all on the same page about this one (you might be surprised to discover that you're actually not).

SHARE WINS

Celebrate wins by sharing them. If you get an email from someone who has grown closer to Christ through your church, don't keep it to yourself. Pass it around to staff members and key volunteers. If you run the children's ministry and you hear a parent share how much his or her child enjoys a teacher, make sure you share it with that teacher. There are wins that should be communicated with the whole congregation from the pulpit, too. Don't keep good news to yourself; make it part of your staff culture or parish life.

ENJOY WINS

Celebrate wins by enjoying them. Carve out a time, a place, and the people who can celebrate with you. Our Monday staff meetings are pretty much only about our weekend wins. It's a meeting that everyone looks forward to (giving them lunch also helps).

Over and over again in the gospels, Jesus is confronted by grumpy religious leaders of his day. Among the very many ways these guys didn't get it was this: They didn't understand what a "win" is in the sight of God. On one occasion, Luke tells us that Jesus took time to try and explain it to them. They still didn't get it, but we can. Know what your wins are, and then, like the inhabitants of heaven, celebrate them.

65

BECAUSE A WIN BELONGS TO EVERYONE

For by grace you have been saved through faith, and this is not from you; it is the gift of God; it is not from works, so no one may boast.

—Ephesians 2:8–9

Tom: Playing sports as a kid, especially football, I remember being grounded in the importance of team. My coaches would say things like "There is no 'I' in team" and "We win as a team; we lose as a team." They were trying to instill in us the lesson that unless everyone's working together, we would not be successful.

That can be difficult to remember as a kid. That can be difficult to remember as an adult, too. While we all have a unique role to play and must fulfill our individual responsibilities in ministry, it is working together that ultimately makes us successful.

One of the draws of sports is that at the end of the game, you know whether you've won or lost, whether you were successful or not. Wins in church work are not always as obvious. As we mentioned in the previous chapter, we define a win as any time a person takes a step on the path of discipleship or any act of faith someone shares with us.

Any win and every step of faith take a team of people. If people hear a message from the altar that changes their hearts, it is only because we had volunteers out on the parking lot to park their cars, greet them at the door, and get them seats. Their conversion of heart comes from within the context of hospitality created by all of our weekend ministers. People get into ministry not only because they have heard it announced clearly, and consistently explained by our staff, but also because they see other parishioners serving with joy and enthusiasm. When a student steps up to the plate to serve on a mission, it's not just our youth minister who deserves the credit, but also dozens of adult leaders who are pouring themselves into the lives of our young people.

The Bible tells us that everything is ultimately grace. In other words, it's really not us; it's God. So, there is no reason to boast about anything we accomplish. But as a leader, how about if you take it a step further? Give other people the credit, as often as you can.

Come to think of it, that is all the time.

66

WHAT GETS REWARDED GETS REPEATED

And everyone who has given up houses or brothers or sisters or father or mother or children or lands for the sake of my name will receive a hundred times more, and will inherit eternal life.

—MATTHEW 19:29

A reward is something given in return for something else, as an encouragement. Money immediately comes to mind, and certainly financial rewards, bonuses and increases, can be great encouragements. Rewards can come in time off, lunches or dinners, gifts, or gift cards.

As human beings, we're naturally attracted to rewards; we like them, we want them, and we seek them. That's not a bad thing: God has hardwired us that way. He encourages us throughout scripture to work for him with that motivation in mind.

The people in your pews who are stepping up to the challenges you're offering them should be rewarded. Your volunteer leaders need to be rewarded. The parish staff must be rewarded. It is the right thing to do and just has to be a part of the culture of your organization.

But there's another reason to do it that is strategic and entirely self-serving: rewards are gifts that keep giving. In an axiom we learned from Pastor Andy Stanley, what gets rewarded gets repeated. If your staff members and volunteer ministers feel valued and appreciated, they will want to work for you and they will be motivated to do more.

People who are uninvolved, parishioners who are disengaged, will notice, and it will motivate them, too. If you thank the people who are serving, more people who aren't serving will step forward and do it. If the people who are providing the financial support of the parish are recognized in some appropriate way, your giving will increase. What gets rewarded gets repeated. Here are some practical steps to take to make it happen. (And please notice that none of these rewards cost you anything.)

THANK PEOPLE PERSONALLY

Catch people working hard, and tell them on the spot that they are doing a good job. Be as specific as you can be in praise. Say, "Thank you for the positive attitude you bring." "Good job working with that child; you really have a gift." "Your contribution to our parish is really making a difference, thanks." When people know specifically what they did well, they will repeat it.

THANK PEOPLE PUBLICLY

Look for opportunities with your current means of communication to thank people publicly. Use your homily; thank people in your announcements, in the bulletin, and even on your website. For example, a parish we know has a volunteer of the month on their home page. Use your e-mail ceaselessly to thank teams of ministers and other volunteers.

THANK STAFF PRIVATELY

Meanwhile, keep your staff rewards internal. By all means, be thanking them all the time; just don't make a big display of thanking one another publicly or asking the congregation to do so. At the congregational level, keep it all about them. A lot of church staffs are way too self-congratulatory, and it's boring.

At one point in the Gospel, a discussion takes place between Jesus and Peter on just this point. Peter argues that he's given up quite a lot to follow Jesus; what will there be for him? Far from correcting his blatant self-interest, in fact, Jesus uses the opportunity to make the bold promise to Peter and all the disciples—a hundred times whatever is given will be given in return, plus eternal life. You have to believe that incentivized them!

67

HAVE FUN

⌃

Rejoice in the Lord always. I shall say it again: rejoice!

—Philippians 4:4

Tom: For the sake of full disclosure, we admit that we are not naturally fun people. Michael's idea of fun is watching cable news while reading the newspaper. As for me, even when I did youth ministry, I was known as "No Fun Corcoran." We are not fun people, nor do we naturally promote or seek fun. It is not our prime motivation in life. So little do we understand fun that in writing this chapter we had to look it up in the dictionary (it means "enjoyment or playfulness"). Obviously, we are by no means experts on this subject.

But, we *are* converts to fun. Our conversion is based on the churches from which we have learned. Rick Warren at Saddleback Church says, "We don't take ourselves seriously, but we take God very seriously."

Leaders at North Point Church like to say, "Where there is no fun, there is soon no one."

While they say these things, their environments match their words. Attending conferences at Saddleback and North Point have always been delightful experiences loaded with humor and hilarity, stuff that simply made us laugh out loud and forced us to enjoy ourselves. As a result, we felt more relaxed and, eventually, more encouraged and inspired.

It's not about entertainment. The Church of Christ is not in the entertainment industry, and the Eucharist should be honored with all possible dignity and devotion. But that doesn't mean your parish has to be only serious or somber.

Fun helps people relax and opens them up to the message of the Gospel. Fun encourages people to know the humanness of that message and that our relationship with God does not mean being serious all the time. God created a sense of humor; laughter was his idea.

Jesus was fun; he was playful. When Peter asked about the Temple tax, Jesus could have paid for it in a hundred different ways. Instead, he told Peter to go fishing and to look for a coin in the mouth of the first fish he caught. It seems he was having some fun. In his first miracle, Jesus turns water into wine, and not just any kind of wine, but rather the choicest vintage. He wanted to have fun. When the Canaanite woman came up to him to heal her daughter, he played with her in a little verbal sparring. Our parishes should reflect the personality of Jesus.

Fun communicates joy in playful ways. If you ever had the opportunity to attend Mass with Pope John Paul II, you know that it was always devout, but also playful (for lack of a better word). The same was true for Mother Teresa. In her approach to ministry, she had a great sense of playfulness.

Some people might push back and say fun is superfluous and unnecessary. So is all of creation. God decided to go ahead and do it anyway. Fun communicates the joy of creation itself as well as the

Christian life, the lightness of heart that comes from a relationship with God. The heart of following Christ is not burden and responsibility but life and joy. Jesus said that he came that we might have life and have it to the full. If we do not have joy and fun in our faith, it could be a sign of spiritual immaturity.

So, how do you integrate fun into your church and weekend worship experience?

LAUGH AT YOURSELF

When we laugh with others we deepen our emotional connection to them. When you get people to laugh at appropriate times during their weekend experience at your church, it helps create community among parishioners and makes newcomers feel more comfortable.

We try to make people laugh during the homily and also after communion at our "Endnotes" (which is what we call the announcements). Chris, our director of student ministry, often does this by referencing the message and then making light of some aspect of it. He regularly pokes fun at the pastor, which is especially helpful if the message has been challenging.

In fact, laughing at oneself is the best place to get started. Sometimes we show videos after Mass (yes, people actually stay to watch them), usually self-deprecating presentations designed to laugh at ourselves and give everyone permission to do the same. Once we made a rap video featuring some of our staff; once we did a takeoff of a popular TV show, making fun of the whole team; and another time, a fake "failed" flash mob suddenly appeared at a conference we were hosting. One Sunday, we had a video making fun of the two of us as the "The Odd Couple." You can have fun out on the parking lot with some unexpected element greeting everyone. Your greeters can all wear silly hats one weekend and get people laughing coming in the front door.

CREATE A FUN ENVIRONMENT

Fun doesn't always mean humor. We have fun when we feel accepted, when we are liked, and when we're around people we like. Fun means guests know they are welcome when we have greeters at the door to welcome them.

We have fun when a presentation engages our attention, and we can simply live in the present moment. We have fun when the music is excellent and lifts our spirits or moves our hearts.

HAVE FUN WITH YOUR STAFF

The staff forms the core of your church, so if your staff has fun, they'll set the tone for everybody else. Again, we are certainly not experts on this, but the fun that we've had at the parish level is a product of the fun we've allowed our staff to enjoy and replicate. Give your staff permission to have fun. Let your staff be creative with it, and you'll be on your way to having a joy-filled church.

St. Paul strikes us as a sort of serious, intense, fun-challenged sort of guy. Yet he tells us that as people of faith, our hearts should be full of joy; we should be rejoicing—always. That sounds like about as much fun as anyone could ever have. It's about joy. There is a joy that springs from faith, which should characterize our lives.

If that's the way we're supposed to be, shouldn't our parishes be that way, too?

OVERALL TOOLS

68

FATHER, IT'S NOT ALL ABOUT YOU

⌄

If you remain in my word, you will truly be my disciples, and you will know the truth, and the truth will set you free.

—John 8:31–32

Father Michael: While Vatican II sought to awaken the universal call to holiness among all believers and the common priesthood of the faithful, the reality of the Catholic culture is that everything drives toward the priest, specifically the pastor— everything. Of course, the sacramental system relies on the priest, who stands in the person of Christ, and at all times exercises a spiritual fatherhood for his parishioners. But does that mean that Father has to chair every meeting he attends, answer every question that is raised, preside over every parish function, provide authentic interpretation for all events, be the only one ever to offer public prayer, always have the first and the last word?

Think about this: According to diocesan procedures currently in place, I am the only one on my staff who can sign checks and I must personally open all mail addressed to the parish. Really? *Really.* Could we discuss the ability of the Church to authorize someone else to open the mail and sign checks?

Our point is this: Everything in the culture insists that the priest be the center of attention, action, activity, and authority: Father is the beginning and the end, the alpha and the omega. Hey, wait a minute, isn't that supposed to be someone else?

Father Michael: When I first came to Nativity, it was thought among the insiders that my presence was needed to validate each and every meeting and any kind of gathering. If I did not attend, whatever was happening was somehow invalid or inauthentic, and people interpreted my absence as a snub or some form of negligence. This feeling went so deep in fact that the expectation wasn't just my attendance but also a kind of pervasive presence at everything. I remember a Christmas party hosted by a parish club one Friday night before Christmas. I stopped by to say hello and work the room and then slipped out. The next morning there was a small delegation in my office to voice their disappointment at my "blowing off" their party.

Over time we have worked to break this conception.

> **Tom:** I remember holding youth events or chairing ministry meetings, and key volunteers would ask me, "Where is Father White, and why isn't he here?" Michael had equipped me to say that as a staff member, I was an extension of his office. Over time, that has become accepted and, now, even expected.

Father, it is not all about you, and that can be a very helpful concept to embrace. It means you don't have to control everything. It means you don't need to attend everything. It means you can go home at night. It means you are free to be human, have time for friends and family.

Here are some practical steps to take in the right direction.

DON'T DOMINATE

Respectfully, but truthfully, this all begins at Mass. Some priests we've seen make it all about them at Mass, constantly inserting themselves into every aspect and detail, micromanaging the proceedings, peppering the text with their own words or providing a running commentary on the action. They are almost screaming, "Look at me." It's understandable; they've been cast in this role, and they're just accepting their part.

Give that up. Except for the homily, try not to dominate during Mass. Humble yourself before the liturgy, melt into the background, and allow Christ to emerge.

Bring as many other voices in as permissible: for the readings, of course, but how about for the weekly announcements and any special ones, too? When others are speaking, please do not do anything to attract attention to yourself; rather, focus on the speaker. Can you reposition your presider's chair so that you are less large and in charge?

DELEGATE RESPONSIBILITY

In your administrative and ministerial offices, delegate responsibility (not just tasks, but also real responsibility) to the right people as often as possible, and trust them. Certainly hold them accountable; insist they remain transparent about their duties as well, but invest them with responsibility and authority. When you do so, you are communicating to the parish that, while you're the leader, there are others who also serve in leadership roles. Support them, encourage them, and get out of their way.

STEP OUT OF THE CENTER

Father Michael: Don't take everything personally (go back and read chapter 63). I will admit that this was a hard lesson to learn and one with which I am still struggling. When you are pouring your heart and soul into something, it's amazingly difficult not to take it personally. But when I do, I am implicitly putting myself at the center of everything. Step out of the center and put Christ there.

It is not all about you, Father; it's about Christ. It's about growing disciples of the Lord Jesus. Accepting and implementing this truth will be liberating for you and for your parish.

69

BE AN AUTHORITY

All power in heaven and on earth has been given to me. Go, therefore, and make disciples.

—MATTHEW 28:18–19

When God created man, he gave him authority over the whole earth. This authority wasn't just power; it was command beyond question; it was sovereignty. When Adam and Eve sinned, they handed over that authority to the devil. Jesus came to fix that, and fix it he did. That's why, before his Ascension into heaven, Jesus said, "All power of authority" is mine.

In other words, he won authority back for humanity. He could do so because he was 100 percent God. But he was also 100 percent man. As God, he exercises authority, he teaches with authority, and he is an authority. As man, he subjects himself to the authority of his heavenly Father. That was crucial to his success; that's how he won authority back.

He placed himself under the authority of his heavenly Father. We see this most clearly played out in the Garden of Gethsemane, where Jesus prays, battles really, to surrender to his Father's will.

> He advanced a little and fell to the ground and prayed that if it were possible the hour might pass him by; he said, "Abba, Father, all things are possible to you. Take this cup from me, but not what I will, but what you will."
>
> —Mark 14:35–36

Here's the point of this mini lesson: Pastors, preachers, and parish leaders (really any kind of leader) should exercise their ministry with authority. Preach with biblical authority, teach with doctrinal authority, and stand with moral authority. We're talking about the authority that is based in the sovereignty of God, the grace of Christ, and the Magisterium of his Church. Our ministry should be based in that authority, and we gain it in a counter-intuitive way—through submission and humility.

> **Father Michael:** Ever notice how some pastors and parish leaders wield authority with a heavy hand but resent and resist any kind of appeal from their bishop? Sure, there can be heavy-handed bishops, too, but as someone who worked for a bishop, I readily attest to the difficult position they're in when it comes to a lot of unhelpful and uncooperative clergy and religious leaders. Probably more than anything, it is a question of attitude.

Here are three attitudes we try to maintain:

- It is not always easy to fulfill all the requests and invitations received from diocesan offices. Sometimes they are inconvenient and unhelpful; sometimes we just can't. But we want to be diligent in trying because we want to be under authority.

- The new edition of the Roman Missal is not an easy adjustment; some of the phrasing is tongue-twistingly tough. We submit to it and its authority.

- Living authentically in all the ways the Church asks us to live (as a priest or as a married man) is challenging and daunting, but we seek to try, and we want our parishioners to know we try.

Consciously and consistently placing ourselves under authority, most of all through the Eucharist and time spent with the Word of God, accesses the authority of God. Be an authority by submitting yourself to it.

70

EVERYTHING TAKES LONGER THAN YOU THINK

The LORD God therefore banished him from the Garden of Eden, to till the ground from which he had been taken.

—GENESIS 3:23

A few years ago, we did a message series about the importance of having extra time and space, beyond the busyness of life. Instead of always pushing ourselves to the limits, we preached the value of living with "margin." We relied on an axiom we learned from others: "Everything takes longer than you think."

Work is just more difficult and time consuming on this side of Adam's sin. Accepting that reality can simply help us be more realistic and less stressed when we're approaching projects. When it comes to our experience as a church, this is definitely true.

We wanted to start a children's nursery program so parents could go to Mass, relax, and actually be able to worship. We thought, "no big deal." Get some volunteer ministers, open up a room, and you are done. It wasn't that easy. It took a great deal of time, energy, and struggle to get our Kidzone to a good place as a healthy and sustainable ministry. When we decided we needed a new sound system, we thought it would be very simple. Pay someone to install it, and you'll be good to go by the weekend, right? Wrong. It took us years to get it working properly.

However difficult we think a project will be, we have a tendency to misunderstand not only how much time it will take, but also how much energy, and unfortunately, how much money will be required.

We have found ourselves consistently underestimating how much is needed to launch programs and undertake projects. This is an important lesson to carry with you, because it can be disappointing and even debilitating to have to learn over and over again.

Here are some practical points to consider.

BE DISCERNING

You need to be judicious in what new projects or programs you take on. Having a solid children's ministry is a tremendous asset. Having a great sound system is absolutely necessary. Don't give them a second thought. On the other hand, there are lots of other things you can get involved in that are not worth your time, but will allure you with the temptation to think, "It won't be that much work." Knowing projects take more energy than we think they will means we need to be more discerning.

BE PATIENT

When you find it difficult to break new ministry ground and you know it matters, don't give up. We remember dozens of times being frustrated and saying, "It shouldn't be this hard." It is hard, especially at the beginning when you are trying to get something established. At times you will become frustrated. That's okay.

BE POSITIVE

Take courage; it isn't you. You are not weird, you are not incompetent, and you are not crazy. You are just coming face-to-face with the reality in which you must operate.

Since the fall of humanity from paradise, life is difficult. Blame it all on Adam and Eve, but nothing is easy. As you already know, that includes church. Making disciples is not easy; reaching the unchurched is not easy. Being the movement Christ wants us to be is not easy. If it were easy, everybody would do it.

71

THERE ARE NO SILVER BULLETS

For the time will come when people will not tolerate sound doctrine but, following their own desires and insatiable curiosity, will accumulate teachers and will stop listening to the truth and will be diverted to myths. But you, be self-possessed in all circumstances; put up with hardships; perform the work of an evangelist; fulfill your ministry.

—2 TIMOTHY 4:3–5

In his crusades against bad guys, the Lone Ranger's calling cards were silver bullets. They became a metaphor for simple, straightforward solutions to complex problems. There is something deep down in human nature that searches for that one magic solution to problem solving. Is there a secret that will solve everything, a shortcut that we've overlooked, or a hidden door others missed?

Maybe you are trying to figure out how to involve people in serving one another instead of just coming to church and acting like consumers. Maybe you are working to gain momentum in your children's ministry or get small groups going. Maybe you're facing a capital campaign and the need to raise a large sum of money. Maybe you're just trying to introduce more people in your community to your church on Sunday morning. If you're like we were, you might be hoping, or at least wishing, that there was an easy, quick solution.

Time and again, we have fallen for finding the one thing that will fix our chronic need for more volunteer ministers, grow our small group program overnight, or instantly improve our staff culture. Over time we have come to learn it can't be done.

When it comes to ministry in your parish, there are no silver bullets. Every major problem and challenge is multifaceted, and because it is, the solution must be multifaceted as well.

The challenges we face and the problems we seek to solve require consistent approaches, focused intensity, and, as we discussed in the last chapter, *time*. Getting people to serve, give, change their lifestyle, or trust you with their money take time. Solving problems requires working in the trenches and understanding the nuances of a situation. Over time you will find the solution.

Paul writes to his protégé Timothy to guide and encourage him in his ministry for the Church in Ephesus. He's well aware that there are plenty of people who are going to be the victims of sloppy, lazy thinking. They want a single solution to every problem, when there are more often several ways to get there. They want to look at the problem as singular and simple, when more often it is multifaceted and complex. They want a "secret solution." There is no secret solution that will solve your problems. The solution will only come through prayer and fasting, discipline, hard work, and perseverance.

There are no silver bullets, and just so you know, the Lone Ranger isn't not real either.

72

SEEK WISE COUNSEL

Moses sat in judgment for the people, while they stood around him from morning until evening. When Moses' father-in-law saw all that he was doing . . . he asked, "What is this business. . . . What you are doing is not wise."

—Exodus 18:13–14, 17

Plans fail when there is no counsel, but they succeed when advisors are many.

—Proverbs 15:22

Often in churchworld, we feel as if we have to know it all. But we don't, we can't, and we don't have to anyway, so we shouldn't pretend we do. One of the ways we can build the Body of Christ and involve more members in the work of the Church is by inviting them to offer their experience and insights. There is much wisdom in our pews if we can tap into it efficiently.

Over the years, we have found counsel in both structured and unstructured ways. We have a parish council and a financial council that are explicitly established to offer their wisdom, insights, advice, caution, and feedback to us. The parish council looks at the totality of parish life, while the financial council, which of course is required by canon law, gives us wisdom in our financial management. We ask our council not only to keep us transparent and accountable with our finances but also to give us their wisdom on how we're spending money, where we're saving (or should be saving), as well as on staffing and salaries.

As we are writing this chapter, we recently attended a very consequential parish council meeting in which consensus was reached on a big decision. We listened to what they had to say and followed their counsel, even though it was not what we wanted to hear.

Over the last few years, we have put together teams to help us with campus planning and a plan to manage our continued growth. We have assembled a team of advisors to look at, and keep looking at, our development efforts and raising up givers in our parish. We have another small team focused on human resources and personnel policies. We have a team that advises and reviews our mission efforts, small-group program, and adult ministry. We would like to add a team for communication, but haven't gotten there quite yet. These are not meetings for the sake of meetings or committees for the sake of committees; this is about seeking wise counsel . . . and following it.

At the same time, we also try to tap into the wisdom around us in less structured, more informal ways. Typically once or twice a week, we sit down over lunch or coffee with successful people in our community and try to learn from them about what they know.

In getting wise counsel, here are three strategies for using the wisdom around you to help your parish go further faster.

CHOOSE WISE ADVISORS

We don't want advice from people who have not been wise with their own lives. In 1 Kings, King Rehoboam sinks the whole nation of Israel into civil war because he asked for the opinion of his friends who had no business advising and no experience in ruling.

Be on the lookout for people whose lives are proof of their wisdom. Look to people who have done well in their careers. Look for people who have successful marriages, solid relationships with their adult children, and form and sustain great friendships.

Seek wise counsel from those who have varied views and diverse backgrounds, not just people like you who happen to agree with you and are going to tell you what you want to hear. It is natural to turn to advisors who are allies, but listen to other voices, too.

LOOK FOR THE SPECIFIC SKILLS AND POINTS OF VIEW

Look for specific skills and points of view out there in the pews. Get wisdom from people with genuine insight, fresh perspectives, and professional experience that match your needs. If you are working on a building program, get counsel from people who own engineering firms or are in the construction business. For another perspective on how your Sunday morning schedule affects families, ask parents with small children.

On the other hand, we've all been part of meetings where parishioners were asked to provide perspective on things (like running a parish or building a ministry) that they didn't know anything about. This wastes our time and theirs. For example, we don't ask our parish council to give much input on how our children's programs or student programs should be run. We know more about it than they do. It isn't their level of expertise. We put that in the hands of our staff and their volunteers who are in the trenches week in and week out. By contrast, we seek a lot of input on our budget.

MAKE THE DECISION

Getting wise counsel doesn't mean you never make a decision. If you are the pastor or the staff person in charge of a project, ultimately you are a decision maker. You have the broadest view, and God has put you in that position. Don't allow counsel to paralyze you into indecision. Get wise counsel; then make a decision and stand behind it.

Over and over again, scripture encourages us to seek wisdom. One of the consistent ways it teaches us to do that is by seeking wise counsel. In Exodus, Moses solves a major problem he's struggling with when he receives the wise counsel of his father-in-law, Jethro. The successful kings of Judah listened to the prophets. In Acts of the Apostles, the gathering of the apostles that is called the Council of Jerusalem ends well, and the mission of the Church expands because Peter and James listened to wise counsel they received there. If they needed it, we probably do, too.

73

CHRISTMAS EVE IS PARADIGM FOR EVERYTHING

∧

They went in haste and found Mary and Joseph, and the infant lying in the manger. When they saw this, they made known the message that had been told them about this child.

All who heard it were amazed by what had been told them by the shepherds. . . .

Then the shepherds returned, glorifying and praising God.

—Luke 2:16–18, 20

Every good business has a research and development department or pilot programs. They're the place for experimentation, by way of trial and error, to see what could be. In his book *Great by Choice*, Jim Collins calls this "firing bullets before cannonballs." Collins uses the analogy of being on an old battleship commencing engagement with an enemy ship, still at a distance. Rather than using all its gunpowder shooting cannonballs at an uncertain target (and missing), the crew fires bullets at the distant ship, adjusts aim, and keeps adjusting aim until the bullets hit. Then, when the target is sure, they start using the cannonballs.

> **Father Michael:** In *Rebuilt*, we tell the story of our decision, at one point, to move off campus on Christmas Eve to a much larger facility nearby where we could accommodate the thousands of people who were coming to us each year on that evening. This began as an attempt to better accommodate the crowds that overwhelmed our facility each Christmas, but unexpectedly, it became an experiment in making church not all about the people already in the pews, but all about the people who aren't usually in the pews.
>
> It was an exercise in seeing if we could change our focus (for one evening anyway) as one of the initial steps in changing our church. It worked, it was a success, and over the intervening years, it has grown considerably (hugely actually).

We've come to rely on the axiom "Christmas Eve is a paradigm for everything." Start somewhere, take aim at some target, and do something, in a smaller way, and then figure out what that taught you about what you want to do in a bigger way.

> **Tom:** In the development of our weekend strategy, we began in a very small way. We introduced a Sunday evening Mass, which at first succeeded in attracting no one but teenagers who had slept in Sunday morning. It was an easy and safe place to

begin using more vibrant (and louder) praise and worship music. It was a natural place to start introducing technology. These elements are now features of our overall experience at all our weekend Masses, but they began at those evening Masses.

Likewise, we used our Vacation Bible School program to set the paradigm for our weekend children's programs. In the beginning, it was much easier for us to create dynamic programs for children during an annual event than trying to do it every Sunday of the year. Our children's team put in a great deal of time and energy creating an excellent presentation and environment. As they did, they learned a lot and built a team of people who came to understand how it could happen in a much bigger way. We don't even do the Bible school anymore, but we've got awesome kids' programs at every Mass, every weekend of the year.

One Lent, we introduced the concept of small groups into our congregation by challenging everyone to get into a group for just six weeks. We used Rick Warren's *40 Days of Purpose* book. Given its popularity, and the limited nature of the commitment, the program was a big hit. It was there we learned about running a parish-wide small-group program. It would still be years before we had even a modest small-group program, but we were on our way.

Father Michael: We confess that not all our pilot programs have been successful. A few years ago, we tried an outreach worship service at a local hotel for unchurched people in our community. We called it Crowne Plaza (because that was the name of the hotel). The idea we used was based on the "Mass of the Catechumenate," a Liturgy of the Word for people who don't otherwise go to

Mass. It had live music and a video message I had prepared in advance.

Tom: I acted as part prayer leader, part MC. It was a fine experience, but it really didn't draw many people. We realized it was burning out our staff and key volunteers who were only going to support us.

While the program didn't translate into a new program, it bore other fruit. We gained new musicians from the experience, because we had to build a new band for the off-campus service. We grew our children's ministry, and the people who helped out at Crowne Plaza continued to do so on our main campus. In fact, our current director of children's ministry started there. We even developed a brand new ministry we had never considered before. The team of guys who got up early to move in and set up at the hotel became our Ops Ministry. Currently they set up and clean up all weekend long.

Pilot programs are crucial for experimenting in a way that will allow you to be creative. They give you permission to take prudent risks in a way that won't bust your budget. And when your programs are successful on a small scale, you will be able to introduce larger changes to your church with confidence and greater ability to answer criticisms and concerns.

Here are some practical steps to take.

START SOMEWHERE

Take a look at one key question or problem your parish is facing right now. Discuss this with your whole staff and major volunteer ministers.

BRAINSTORM

Begin brainstorming about what you can do to test out a possible solution that could be the way forward. There are no bad ideas getting started.

GIVE YOURSELF PERMISSION TO FAIL

When you decide what to do, undertake it with all the necessary energy and resources available, but also with the understanding that it might not work, and it will be okay if it doesn't. If it fails, don't look at it as a waste of time or money, but as an investment in your education as a leader. Learn from the lesson and move on to plan B.

The story of the Nativity, as related in the Gospel of Luke, presents in microcosm the whole mystery of the Incarnation. The purposes Christ invests in the Church are on display in a single evening. It is a scene full of truth and grace, and animated by worship, fellowship, ministry, mission, and evangelization. At its heart, there is Christ himself. That first Christmas became a paradigm for everything that followed. Where is your potential paradigm?

74

IT'S NOT AN AIR WAR; IT'S A TRENCH WAR

The Lord appointed seventy-two others whom he sent ahead of him in pairs to every town and place he intended to visit. He said to them, "Whatever town you enter and they welcome you, eat whatever is set before you, cure the sick in it and say to them, 'The kingdom of God is at hand for you.'"

—Luke 10:1–2, 8–9

Even though all is not well in the Catholic Church these days, we've been here before. One particularly low point came in the early twelve hundreds: Rome was addicted to intrigue, belabored by scandal, besieged by enemics, and plagued by intractable problems. At just about that time, a young man, who desired greatly only to serve God, sought divine guidance in the wreck of a ruined little chapel near the Italian town of Assisi. There, God spoke clearly, simply instructing him, "Francis, repair my house, which, as you can see, is falling into ruin." With arresting obedience, St. Francis lost no time in undertaking the request; literally, he began repairing the chapel where he found himself that day. That turned out to be the first step in a period of amazing renewal for the whole Church.

Obviously, God wanted Francis to lead the way forward in rebuilding the Church universal, not just the Church of San Damiano. Yet, Francis has much to teach us in his simple approach. He didn't worry about issues beyond his purview; rather, he focused on the problems before him. He saw the rubble he was standing amid and did something about that. He did what he could do about what needed to be done where he was.

We have come to realize that the renewal of the Church is a trench war, not an air war. Although it can sound trite, or like a code word for a certain political agenda, the Church is the People of God, as the Second Vatican Council taught us. It is made of living stones. The renewal and rebuilding of the universal Church begins as we rebuild our local churches by the building up of our parishes, stone-by-stone and heart-by-heart.

While all renewal must be under the supervision and authority of the magisterium in a bond of willing ascent and charity, true renewal also begins in the hearts of believers and the communities of our parishes. The Church will be renewed as individual lives and hearts are changed and become more fully devoted followers of Christ and, in turn, as parishes are more and more changed. In this sense, it is easy to appreciate that serving in a parish—deep in the trenches—is the most important work on earth.

Recorded only in the Gospel of Luke, we read about Jesus' basic strategy of evangelization. He impacted the territory of Judea by covering it with messengers, traveling two-by-two into each town and village—a practice continued by the early Church.

The renewal of the Church will come when enough people get serious about digging in the trenches and getting to work there. Do the little things around you, and do them well. Serve in the simple, unremarkable, little noted, little noticed trenches of parish life. Stay there. Be content to stay there. Flourish there and be fruitful, and know that if you are faithful, if you work hard and work wisely, God will change lives. You do the little things; he will do big things.

75

STOP TRYING TO MAKE PEOPLE GO TO CHURCH, AND MAKE CHURCH MATTER

The kingdom of heaven is like a treasure buried in a field, which a person finds and hides again, and out of joy goes and sells all that he has and buys that field. Again, the kingdom of heaven is like a merchant searching for fine pearls. When he finds a pearl of great price, he goes and sells all that he has and buys it.

—Matthew 13:44–46

A friend of ours recounted a meeting he attended with a group of pastors. One pastor stood up and said, "How do we make people go to church?" We understand that point of view. We're churchpeople, so we think people should be going to church every weekend. However, the days of people going to church out of obligation, guilt, or just to get their mother-in-law off their backs are over. We can't make people go to church. The argument from authority pretty much went out of style in the Enlightenment, and it has finally caught up with the Catholic Church. Just because we're the Church doesn't mean we can make people do anything, and we shouldn't want to anyway.

People are walking away, and staying away, from the Church in droves; that is a fact. That doesn't mean they're bad people, or even that they don't believe in God. On the Sundays following 9/11 or, more recently, Newtown, churches across the country were filled. But they emptied out again quickly, for the same reason they were empty to begin with. We're boring and bad; we're irrelevant in people's lives, and whenever we're given the chance, like a national tragedy or a major holiday, we just prove it all over again.

We're spending all our time thinking about, plotting and scheming, or coaxing and commanding them to come to church, but we never even stop to consider that we don't have anything to offer them (at least anything that they want). We should be putting more thought and time into how we can make them want to come to church and want to come back.

People are hungering for more than what this world offers. They know that the things of this world do not satisfy their hearts. They know that more money, more entertainment, more sex, and more pleasure do not satisfy. At the same time, they've just given up on the Church's ability to answer their questions, offer solutions to their problems, or prove in any way relevant to their lives.

Most people are not far from God because they want to be. They've just wandered off in that direction. They are lost sheep, and rather than be the shepherds we're called to be, we've just let them wander off.

We can be a generation that reverses that trend and changes the tide, if and when we start living up to our calling. Rather than trying to make anybody do anything, how about if we create environments people want to be a part of? We can be sharing with them how the Word of God can help us live better, more successful lives and how church fellowship can provide support for our daily struggles. We can help them come to know the Eucharist as the life-giving food of God that brings us Christ and can shape us into his Body.

We're not here to make people fulfill an obligation. The Church exists to reach out to the world and bring people into a growing relationship with Jesus Christ. In the process, hearts can be healed, marriages saved, relationships restored, families made whole again, addictions overcome, anger abated, joy renewed, hope dawn, and love rule. God is inviting our help in building healthy Catholic parishes of growing disciples who are falling in love with Jesus Christ.

The movement of the kingdom of God is the great treasure, and people who discover it gladly give up everything to gain it. There is nothing more important than this movement because it is the movement of love, and it is the fundamental work of our parishes.

Start loving people, beginning with those far from God; help them fall in love with God, and then just wait and see what happens. You'll have to lock the front doors to keep them out.

Father Michael: I remember watching a service from one of the fastest-growing churches in the country, under the direction of one of the youngest and perhaps most successful pastors anywhere,

Pastor Steve Furtick of Elevation Church in Charlotte, North Carolina. Pastor Steve ended the service with these simple words: "I love you."

Try it once.

Michael White received his bachelor's degree from Loyola University Maryland and his graduate degrees in sacred theology and ecclesiology from the Pontifical Gregorian University in Rome. After being ordained a priest of the Archdiocese of Baltimore, he worked for five years as personal secretary to William Cardinal Keeler, who was then archbishop. During that time, White served as the director of the papal visit of Pope John Paul II to Baltimore.

During his tenure as pastor at Church of the Nativity, the church has almost tripled in weekend attendance from 1,400 to more than 4,000. More importantly, the commitment to the mission of the Church has grown, evidenced by the significant increase of giving and service in ministry. White is coauthor of *Rebuilt: Awakening the Faithful, Reaching the Lost, and Making Church Matter*.

Tom Corcoran received his bachelor's degree from Loyola University Maryland and studied graduate level theology at Franciscan University of Steubenville. Corcoran has served Church of the Nativity in a variety of roles that give him a unique perspective on parish ministry and leadership. Beginning as a youth minister, Corcoran later held positions as coordinator of children's ministry and director of small groups. He currently serves in the position of associate to the pastor and is responsible for weekend message development, strategic planning, and staff development. Corcoran is coauthor of *Rebuilt: Awakening the Faithful, Reaching the Lost, and Making Church Matter*.

"If you love your parish, read this book."

From the foreword by **Cardinal Timothy M. Dolan**
Archbishop of New York

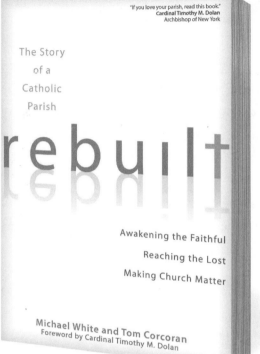

"If you love your parish, read this book."
Cardinal Timothy M. Dolan
Archbishop of New York

The Story
of a
Catholic
Parish

rebuilt

Awakening the Faithful

Reaching the Lost

Making Church Matter

Michael White and Tom Corcoran
Foreword by Cardinal Timothy M. Dolan

320 pages, $16.95, Also available as an eBook.

Does Fr. Michael White and lay associate Tom Corcoran's portrait of their breaking-down parish sound familiar? **Boring weekend Masses** with **snooze-worthy** preaching and **painful music, lackluster buildings, dormant** youth ministry programs, **tepid stewardship, complaining parishioners,** and— worst of all—**waning membership.**

Rebuilt
Awakening the Faithful, Reaching the Lost, Making Church Matter
Michael White and Tom Corcoran

Rebuilt is a story of stopping everything and changing focus. Fr. White and Tom Corcoran reveal how they gleaned wisdom from thriving megachurches and innovative business leaders, anchored their vision in the Eucharistic center of Catholic faith, and brought their parish back to life. Their vision and strategies are presented here with a wealth of guidance for anyone with the courage to hear it.

To Order:
(800) 282-1865
www.avemariapress.com

AVE | AVE MARIA PRESS
A Ministry of the United States
Province of Holy Cross